DIASPORIC EXPERIENCES OF ROHINTON MISTRY AND HIS NOVELS

DIASPORIC EXPERIENCES OF ROHINTON MISTRY AND HIS NOVELS

Nisha Tyagi
(Ph.D. Scholar)

ABHIJEET PUBLCATIONS
NEW DELHI 110002

ABHIJEET PUBLICATIONS
4658-A, First Floor, Ambika Bhawan,
21 Ansari Road, New Delhi 110002
Phone: 011-23259444
E-mail: abhijeetpublication@gmail.com
twitter:- @AbhijeetPub21
whatsapp:- 8076785356
instagram: @abhijeet_publications
LinkedIn: jitendra-singh-7729292b/

DIASPORIC EXPERIENCES OF ROHINTON MISTRY AND HIS NOVELS

First Published 2021

ISBN 978-81-953707-9-5

PRINTED IN INDIA

Published by J.K. Singh for Abhijeet Publications, New Delhi-110002, Lasertypeset by Abhijeet Typesetters, New Delhi and Printed at Milan Enterprises, New Delhi.

DIASPORIC EXPERIENCES OF ROHINTON MISTRY AND HIS NOVELS

Nisha Tyagi
(Ph.D. Scholar)

ABHIJEET PUBLCATIONS
NEW DELHI 110002

ABHIJEET PUBLICATIONS
4658-A, First Floor, Ambika Bhawan,
21 Ansari Road, New Delhi 110002
Phone: 011-23259444
E-mail: abhijeetpublication@gmail.com
twitter:- @AbhijeetPub21
whatsapp:- 8076785356
instagram: @abhijeet_publications
LinkedIn: jitendra-singh-7729292b/

DIASPORIC EXPERIENCES OF ROHINTON MISTRY AND HIS NOVELS

First Published 2021

ISBN 978-81-953707-9-5

PRINTED IN INDIA

Published by J.K. Singh for Abhijeet Publications, New Delhi-110002, Lasertypeset by Abhijeet Typesetters, New Delhi and Printed at Milan Enterprises, New Delhi.

Dedicated to

my grandparents, parents and loving siblings

Grand Parents:	Late Shri Shankar Narayan Tyagi Late Smt. Ganga Devi
Parents:	Shri Bhudev Singh Tyagi Smt. Susheela Tyagi
Siblings:	Mrs. Anuradha Sagar Mrs. Anita Varun Mr. Umesh Tyagi

Acknowledgements

First of all, I offer my sincere thanks to Almighty for giving me strength to pursue this mighty task of writing this book.

I thank my loving parents for spiritually guiding me, helping me to locate varied libraries placed in Delhi having the relevant research material; for late night teas and snacks to keep me awake; for their unconditional support, love and encouragement. Any words of thanks could not suffice their sacrifice and love. I bow and thank them from the bottom of my heart.

I would like to express my gratitude to my mentor Dr. Shweta Singh, Assistant Professor, Amity Institute of English Studies and Research, Amity University, for her guidance, constant motivation and encouragement which always provided an impetus to my research work. I could not have imagined having a better advisor and mentor. I heartly thank her for her constant support of inspiration throughout this journey.

Last but not the least, I would like to thank and express my gratitude to all libraries, especially Sahitya Academy, New Delhi, which facilitated to write valuable information in this book.

NISHA TYAGI

Contents

Chapter One

Introduction

The premise of this Book is to discuss the Diasporic experiences in Rohinton Mistry's books, *Tales from Firozsha Baag, Such a Long Journey* and *A Fine Balance.* Diaspora is a Greek word which gives a sense of *"**scattering of seeds**"*. According to Cohen (1997), the significance of this term is that when a person migrates from one place to other, one country to other or one geographical region to other then he or she becomes a victim of the ignorance. The feeling of ignorance makes the migrants feel like a second creature in the foreign land. It becomes very difficult for them to find their own identity in the exile. They suffer from identity crisis, feel insecure and often have a feeling of conflict between motherland and land of their workplace.

According to Steven Vertovec, diaspora has three significances which are (i) ***it is a social form,*** (ii) ***it is a consciousness and*** (iii) ***it is a mode of***

cultural production (Vertovec, 5). All three diaspora has different notions: first, the social form of diaspora mainly discusses the alienation & loss and tells us how migrants deal with these feelings. Second, diaspora as a consciousness discusses about the migrants' dilemma between here (one place) and there (another place). The concept of here and there gives rise to many difficulties for migrants to become a part of the host country. Lastly, cultural production diaspora is different in comparison to the rest two notions. It basically deals with cultural hybridity, which means migrants leave their homes for better perspectives in life but they feel nostalgic in another country.

Diaspora literature is concerned with two types of relationships: one with the motherland which gives rise to nostalgia and memories, and second with the adopted country and its people which gives rise to conflicts and split personalities. Migrants not only differentiate with their roots but they also scatter on many another terms like language, history, society, individuals, culture, customs and traditions in the host country. According to R.K. Jain, diaspora has two factors: pull and push factors and both have different meanings and impacts on peoples. The push factor signifies lack of employment, business opportunities, political rights, historical upheavals, arrest, punishment, terrorism, corruption and military expulsion. The pull factor signifies the cheap purchase of farmland and better welfare programs. It shows that sometimes they become migrant forcefully and sometimes for better perspectives in life.

Diaspora was started to be seen as a movement of Jews specifically who were exiled to Babylonia from Israel in 607 BC and it is referred as a Jewish Diaspora. Later on, it was seen through Indentured Labor when Africans were exported to the West as slaves. After the Second World War, migration became voluntary and a global phenomenon. Diaspora literature has covered different kinds of the diasporas viz. African, Asian, European, North American, Oceanian and Internal diaspora. Robin Cohen, in his book *"Global Diaspora"* has divided these diasporas in five terms:

1) **Victim Diaspora:** This explains about the members of the community who have migrated from their birthplace. It gives rise to enslavement and exile. Example: Africans.

2) **Trading Diaspora:** It refers to the members of those communities who migrated abroad for trading. The host country Government permitted them to use their local language and rituals, but they could not assimilate. Example: Armenians, Chinese and Jews.

3) **Imperial Diaspora**: It talks about members of those communities who were migrated to another land by their own nation. They

could not adopt the customs and language of host country. Example: Spanish.

4) **Labor Diaspora:** It explains about the members of those communities who migrated for the indentured labor through the agreement in host countries. These peoples were called by the names of labor migrants and indentured servants. Example: Indentured Indians.

5) **De territorialized Diaspora**: It refers to the members of those communities who migrated to another country, but became unknown for another community. In today's era, the population of such communities is decreasing day by day. Example: The Caribbean, Sindhis and Parsees.

Moreover, migration of Indians has been examined in three ways which are: ancient and medieval, colonial and post-colonial. In ancient and medieval phase, we see that from ages Indians have been migrating to different parts of the world. The phase of colonial period deals with those Africans who sailed towards the West as slaves. However, most of our literature talks about Indian diaspora which basically deals with those peoples who emigrated during the colonial period, especially during the 1830s to 1930s.

Diasporic Writers:

There are certain prominent names representing

Indian diasporic experiences such as V.S. Naipaul, Salman Rushdie, Anita Desai, Firdaus Kanga, Amitav Ghosh, Bharti Mukherjee and Veena Singh. They all are diasporic writers who write about their nation and home. Diasporic authors use the common themes of alienation, loneliness, rootlessness, exile, displacement, dislocations, issue of identity, cultural conflicts, emergency etc. Through these, they share their common knowledge of history, culture and experiences of rejection by the host country in their writings.

All these diasporic writers have common themes but they all come under one eternal theme ***"sense of displacement"***. This theme leaves these writers in search of home and transformation of identities because they not only deal with the issues of geographical dislocation but they also have concern for the socio – cultural issues. So many critical thinkers like Sudesh Mishra and Sushil Kumar in their paper, ***"Sugar to Masala: Writing by the Indian Diaspora"***, observe that they are not Indian citizens but global citizens.

Vidiadhar Surajprasad Naipaul was born in 1932 and has achieved Noble Laureate prize. His name appears first in the list of diasporic writers. He is a Hindu Brahmin by birth and has spent his childhood in Trinidad. His grandparents had spent many years as indentured laborer's, working for plantation during the time of British Empire. Thus, sense of homelessness became part of his life and most of his writing speaks about it. He has written many novels out of which ***'House for Mr. Biswas'*** is quite famous, published in 1961. The main character in the novel, Mr. Biswas when he leaves the Tulsi home and starts finding a new home, explains an act of finding a belongingness. Thus, it can be said that diasporic writers lead their life in search of belongingness.

Salman Rushdie is another famous name for diasporic writing, born on 19th June 1947 in Bombay. His parents moved to Pakistan in 1967 and Rushdie was never accepted whole heartedly in Pakistan. He also uses the sense of displacement in his writings. He makes his debut in literature by ***'Grimus'*** but another novel, ***'Midnight's Children'*** became very famous. His works deals with the theme of alienation. In *Grimus*, the central character Flapping Eagle starts to live in a new country and feels alienated because the host country is different from his homeland. He alienates on various issues including culture, language, dressing style and much more. He tries to assimilate but failed. Rushdie also said whole assimilation is not the end because the feelings of alienation and dislocation are permanent.

Another name in the list of diasporic writers is Amitav Ghosh, who was born in Calcutta on July 11, 1956. He moved to Delhi for higher studies and at present he lives in New York. ***'Sea of Poppies'*** is a tremendous work of him which was published in 2008. The novel basically sheds the light on the colonial period and first wave of migration of indentured laborers. Ghosh mainly deals with the historical and political upheavals of first generation of workers who left their homeland and never returned. His writing mainly deals with their identity crisis and belongingness. It can this be said that all diasporic writers have common themes but they use different ways to explain their feelings.

Indian diaspora acts as a ***"bridge between two countries"***. Regarding writings of different diasporic writers, we can say that they cannot come out of their birth place, where they spent their childhood, where they made lots of memories. All these memories, identity crisis, dislocation make them nostalgic.

Subsequently, one can also see the clash between old and new diaspora. These authors divided the diaspora between first and the current generation. First generation people were attached with their motherland and felt the nostalgia in exile land. They experienced the life of an alien over there. But the current generation diaspora is different because this is based on globalization. They feel to accommodate in the exile land and get better opportunities over there.

I would like to share a new meaning of globalization here. We all are living in the world of metropolitan cities which are very fast and forward moving. Globalization has introduced many new things to us like foreign companies, malls, Mc Donald's, Coffee–Costa, Café Coffee Day brands etc. It is a fact that because of advent of these brands in our country the recession has gone, many students and people got jobs, individuals are earning their bread and butter by this, but still, they all are foreign brands and we are dependent on it. So, my perspective is that we are directly and indirectly dependent and colonized by these brands.

Indian–Canadian Diaspora:

The Indian–Canadian diaspora is also a branch of Diasporic literature. It refers to the people who have migrated to Canada from India. In this situation, a person is spiritually and psychologically divided between two nations. Indian-Canadian diaspora is not new in literature. The first Indian–Canadian novelist is **Sadhu Singh Dhami** and he wrote the first Indo–Canadian text, ***'Maluka'***. The main protagonist of the novel hails from Punjab and the story depicts the migrants of Punjab in Canada and how they tried to adapt the new culture. It is true that the Indians who migrated to Canada faced many emotional and physical trauma because their world had changed.

Literature of Indo–Canadian sheds light on the contemporary issues which directly deal with the history, geography, culture and economics. When immigrants went to the Canada for a better life, they explored for better jobs in esteemed companies like Canadian Pacific Railway and Hudson Bay. With the help of these jobs, their backbone became strong on economic standards. Both India and Canada are multicultural nations. India is also a country where so many different ethnic community people live together and make history. There is a hybridity of cultures and languages.

Moreover, the authors of Indian-Canadian diaspora has chosen the major issues of identity by tagging different names in their works. There are several stereotypes like black people in the United States were tagged as ***"Negroes"***, East Indians were tagged as ***"Pakis"***, Jews as ***"Kiles"*** and Chinese as ***"Chinks"***. This victimization makes them nostalgic. If we call people with another name or tag them with another identity, it is an act of humiliation and domination. Through this, the person starts feeling the contrast between the present and past.

We have got several examples of Indian–Canadian diasporic literature, for instance ***'No New Land'*** by M.G Vassanji, ***'Can You Hear the Night Bird Call'*** by Anita Rau Badami, ***'Voyage of Komagata Maru'*** by Prof Hugh Johnston and ***'Trishanku'*** by Uma Parmeshwaram, and with literature these writers have discussed and debated the dilemma of diaspora. Through their writing, they opine that diaspora makes bridge between two nations. Though they all have different notions of writing but their pain and sufferings of migration are similar.

Introducing Writer, Themes and his Religion

Rohinton Mistry was born on July 3, 1952, moved to Canada from Mumbai in 1975 and has been living there since then. He is an Indian-Canadian, an exiled Indian Parsee. We can say that he is Zoroastrian by faith and Persian (Iranian) by their origin. He completed his education in Mathematics Hons from St. Xavier College from Mumbai in 1974, he also continued his studies in Toronto after the migration and took the degree of English and Philosophy Hons in part-time mode from the Toronto University in 1982. He is a victim of double–displacement as his ancestors first migrated to India and later, he migrated to Canada. He is a short story critic and an author. He now lives in Toronto but his heart beats for Parsees. He sets his books on local Mumbai and through his work he displays an adoring picture of India.

Mistry is an author of the Indian diaspora and his migration deals with the phase of second Asian diaspora. He achieved tremendous recognition as a literary figure with just only four books. He is extremely concerned with the history in a similar way like Salman Rushdie, Kushwant Singh, and Nayantara Sehgal depict their own emotions through their works. He has an exceptional sensibility, a delicate corner for the discouraged and innocent individuals. He is brilliant in capturing the crowd and throbbing lives of Indians in his writing. His works analyze the common issues:

self, place, identity and community of post-colonial time.

Moreover, he examines the historical events and expresses how the individuals' lives get affected in post–independent period. Mistry's writings are uniquely based on real facts from history. He deals with Parsee community, connects the text with post–independent Indian history. His work constitutes both, facts and fiction. He said, in post–independence time the nation was divided, first divided between the religion and language and secondly divided between caste and classes. These caste and religion clashes left a bad impact on social institutions. The result came out that everyone's heart got full with disaffection for everyone and it became a part of the day-to-day life. He shares his opinion that human being is a social animal and whatever happens, makes a social pressure on him and continue by saying that directly and indirectly, one has to adopt the social milieu. He further said about the untouchables that society starts behaving like uneducated and inhuman with them.

Mistry has started his writing with short stories, ***Tales from Firozsha Baag,*** and his three books, ***Such a Long Journey, A Fine Balance*** and ***Family Matters***. Through his writing, he places himself in an opposing post-colonial era and sentiment which is indeed a myth that bests suit to the reason. The component of diasporic emotions in this study has managed the issue by adjusting the grandness of myth with the most basic method of reality.

Therefore, diasporic writers share the perspectives about how their community gets neglected. These novelists have depicted their pattern of society through symbols and images. They not only enlighten about their communities past, but also present the kaleidoscopic picture about these issues and subject. The list of these postcolonial writers includes many names like Salman Rushdie, Amitav Ghosh and Shashi Tharoor who have used these subjects in their Indian fiction in English. They all have re–narrated the history of their religion, community and country. For example, Rohinton Mistry has shown his main concern for Parsee community in particular and others in general.

These writers become the favourite of their country by their writings and gained acclaim in the hearts of the readers, listeners and critics. They raise the voice for the anxieties, fear, hopes and yearnings of their community. Such ethnic minority who has migrated in different parts of the world, has to face the multicultural pressure over there. At the time of post-modernism the concept of writing has changed from centre to margins. History has witnessed that many minority communities migrated in other parts of the world.

Parsee community is the best example of migration who had migrated from Persia (Iran) to India in the 7th century. They first become the part of Sanjan in Gujarat, later they settled in Bombay and other parts of the world. They became victim of migration and faced many challenges in their life. They first faced the situation of quest for identity and second, they fell in for the difficulties to maintain their cultural identity. The remarkable feature about the Parsees is their patience and adaptability. They set a good example about their strength because they adopt and assimilate in the cultural society in India. The cultural anxieties become the themes of the Parsees writers. Rohinton Mistry is not the only one example of Parsee immigrant. Whenever we talk about Parsee writers, Bapsi Sidhwa's name comes along with Mistry's name. She is also a Parsee expatriate and they both write about their community.

The Zoroastrian Persian Empire migrated under the effect of Muslims during 638 AD and 641 AD. The community of Parsees is recognized as a calm, hardworking and peaceful community. They have had fights for their rights but they were forcefully migrated from their birth land. They met with thrashing and needed to escape from Madyan (in their nation Iran) to make their homes in different nations. Owing similarity to many features and hospitality, India gave shelter of security to these displaced people.

In eighth century, they came to Diu and stayed here for a long time. At that point, they cruised towards Gujarat and arrived at the port of Sanjan. The neighborhood leader of Sanjan, Jadav Rana, permitted them to stay there on two conditions first, they had to mix with Indian community like sugar in milk and second, they would not use Indian's language and dressing style. As they did not adapt these conditions, they were called Parsees in light of the fact that the language they talked was ***'Farsi'***. After the Mughals gained power in India, they introduced the Persian language. This furnished the Parsees with some comfort and solace in having their vernacular restored to them.

Many authors have given their perspectives on Parsees like Kushwant Singh in his book ***'India an Introduction'*** has described many major and minor things about Zoroaster religions. He said they have good and bad Gods: Ahura Mazda belongs to the category of good and wise soul and contrary to it, Angra Mainyu is the evil and bad spirit. The holy books of Zoroaster are called ***"Gathas"*** and Zenda Avesta is a holy book in their religion (Singh, 3). The word "Agiaries" is a symbol of a temple where they worship their gods. Nilofer Bharuch in her book ***'Reflection in Broken Mirrors: Diverse Diaspora in Recent Parsees Fiction'*** says:

"It is a dying community: the rate of death is higher

Then the rate of birth: they admit no converts nor

Recognize offspring of non–Parsee's father as Parsees" (Bharuch, 6)

Through above lines she has given a view about the Parsees population. She said that in the last decade of 20th century, 70,000 Parsees lived in India, Europe and North America and rest in Iran and Pakistan.

The Parsees are personally associated with the historical backdrop of Bombay. The cotton blast was to a great extent fruitful in light of Parsees business visionaries. The most established daily paper in Bombay, ***Bombay Samachar,*** was controlled by them. One of India's greatest modern houses established by them was that by Jamshedji Tata. A large number of Bombay thoroughfares, streets and structures were constructed by them. In our history, there are a number of established names who are Parsees and have achieved name and fame. Some of the notable names are Dada Bhai Nauroji, Dinshaw Wacha and Feroz shah Mehta.

Justification of Rohinton Mistry and his works

I have chosen Rohinton Mistry because he writes about tribes and tribulations. His writing depicts historical and political India with the questions of identity crisis, past location, nostalgia, and uncovers his whole consciousness about his excursion of Parsee identity. He uses India as a whole in his novels and identity as theme. I have chosen his three of his novels, ***Tales from Firozsha Baag, Such a Long Journey*** and ***A Fine Balance***. The novels are based on politics, history and identity crisis. Mistry uncovers many delicate issues of his community in his writing. This Book reflects his identity issues and dislocation that has been spread across Six chapters covering introduction of topic, writer, background of themes and novels.

The first chapter is Introduction about author, themes and his texts.

The Second chapter Critical analysis of portrayal of historical and political upheavals of India in Rohinton Mistry Context. This will discuss the political and historical background of India and reflect how the community and society were affected at the time of emergency, post–independence and how they lose their identity.

The Third chapter is Critical analysis of caste and community imbalances of India in Rohinton Mistry Context. It discusses the internal emergency with caste and communism of India and reflects how the ordinary people become the victim of identity crisis and at last they start to search their identity.

The Fourth Chapter Critical analysis of narrative techniques of Rohinton Mistry in Indian Context which will discuss his techniques and style of storytelling, geographical description, the way he uses his themes, issues about his home and locale.

The Fifth chapter Critical analysis of Rohinton Mistry work in Indian Context which will discuss about the Rohinton Mistry's perspective about all books into the Indian Context.

The sixth chapter is Conclusion and it will conclude whole chapters with my perspectives.

Background of Novels

Mistry's first published work, from the year 1987, *Tales from Firozsha Baag* is a collection of 11 short stories that are structured on the themes of identity crisis, alienation, community, and the self. The stories revolve around the everyday lives of a Parsee-dominated housing complex in Bombay called Firozsha Baag. The characters deal with the crisis and conflicts rising within and around the Parsee families as they struggle to hold onto their traditions while trying to assimilate themselves into the big city life of a post-colonial India, as members of a religious minority. Interestingly, toward the end of the book, though briefly, Mistry's life takes the center stage as the story shifts to the experiences of Indian Parsees facing double displacement, after having moved to countries like Canada and the United States. *Tales from Firozsha Baag* won Mistry the first prize in the Hart House Literary Contest for two consecutive years, in 1983 and 1984, as well as the Annual Contributor's Prize presented by the Canadian Fiction Magazine, in 1985.

Such a Long Journey is written by Rohinton Mistry and published in 1991. Sturla Gunnarsson was so much influenced by this novel that he made a movie on this. The movie was made in 1998 and screenplay was written by Sooni Taraporevala. The novel is based on tales of common Bombayites talking about the main character, Gustad's life and his hard works. He is a family man and his family and other characters' lives get haunted throughout the novel during War of China in 1962. Mistry sets the background with Indo-Pak war and uses ordinary man and women as the protagonists. Henceforth his characters are not hero but they fight with situations very heroically. *Such a Long Journey* has written his name in the list of prominent diaspora writers. He won numerous honors, viz. Canada's Governor General's Award for fiction, the Commonwealth Author's Award for the Best Book of the Year, and the WH Smith Books in Canada First Novel Honor. It was likewise named for the UK-based Booker Prize (now known as the Man Booker).

A Fine Balance, the second novel by Mistry was published in 1995 which won a few honors including the Commonwealth Writers Prize, the prestigious Giller Prize, Los Angeles Time Book Prize for Fiction and The Royal Society of Literature's Winifred Hotly Award. He has also achieved Booker Prize (for his first novel), the International *IMPAC* Dublin Scholarly Award, and the Irish Times International Fiction Prize. This very famous novel tells the story of characters Dina, Om, Ishwar and Maneck and their lives during Emergency. A very interesting aspect shown from beginning to end in the novel is train. The story starts with stopping of a train and also ends with the same. The novel and characters are very powerful and author portrays harsh reality of politics and politicians.

Tales from Firozsha Baag, Such a Long Journey and *A Fine Balance,* represent the delicate subjects and issues of migration and double-displacements. The settings of these books are based on history and politics, social, caste and cultural imbalances and religion of India. Mistry depicts how these facets are embraced by the characters of the novel. He also portrays the household life and social life as a family unit. He indicates how the text speaks to the significance of home in the development of society and social talks about class, caste, family and personality.

While *Tales from Firozsha Baag* engages with the overwhelming question of communal identity, *Such a Long Journey* and *A Fine Balance,* both throw the light on history of India and depict how history and politics get interlinked with each other, for example Emergency, Sikh riots, Indo-Pak war, Indo–China War and War of Bangladesh.

Mistry has portrayed his characters in a simple and sophisticated way to tackle the political and social circumstances which put them into a stiff situation about the public and personal personality. In *Tales from Firozsha Baag,* Mistry has brought to light the struggles in the everyday lives of the residents of a housing complex in Bombay. Largely focusing on the dominant group residing there, Mistry has presented the challenges faced by the Parsees as they try to make sense of their new place in a post-colonial India, navigating their way through an overburdening identity crisis. *Such a Long Journey* has raised questions about the trust, friendship and loyalty about the characters' language and their communication in the atmosphere of political and corrupted nation. *A Fine Balance* has been set during the hard time of Emergency which was declared by the Prime Minister Mrs. Indira Gandhi. This novel is also filled with the subject of corruption and politics.

Therefore, the research will discuss and think about the experiences and consciousness of diaspora in Rohinton Mistry with his three novels, *Tales from Firozsha Baag, Such a Long Journey* and *A Fine Balance.* It will discuss political and historical upheavals, caste and community imbalances etc. These topics are the sensitive issues which talk about self and others, center to margin and periphery. It deals with the sufferings related to identity and quest for identity. Many critical viewers have given different views on Mistry's writings. For instance, Vinod Kumar says that in modern era, diaspora is different, the notion of diaspora is different. He says migrants are in a dilemma between the being and belongingness. People want to achieve something prominent in life, so they leave their birthplace and take a new step for becoming something prominent and conclude with the things waiting to be explored. Authors like Vijay Lakshmi. M, Meera Vasani, Nidhi Gupta etc. have some different perspectives on it. They say that it deals with identity, talks about religion, and shows his nostalgia about India through his writings. They all appreciated Mistry and his works. Another critical thinker Krishanu Adhikari is greatly influenced by his style of writing.

But the present research will be different from the available corpus of knowledge on diasporic experiences in Rohinton Mistry novels. The research that has been done till now is not in a proper literary form and the present research will give a proper insight into the study of diasporic experiences in Rohinton Mistry's *Tales from Firozsha Baag, Such a Long Journey* and *A Fine Balance*. It will reflect the true image of history, culture, community, politics and caste in Indian literature. This research work will bring out the immense richness and positive vibes to the diaspora. By this work, we will see another side of diaspora.

Chapter Two

Critical Analysis of Historical and Political Upheavals of India in Rohinton Mistry Context

Such a Long Journey is filled with sounds, smells and colours of India and shows different sights and author depicts the sentiments of small Parsee community. In the present time, their population is getting lesser and they are introvert in their nature. When we go through the story of the novel, we realize that the characters are neither sinners nor saints. The author through his work gives the feeling about the problems and issues of their culture to the readers. *Such a Long Journey* goes around the protagonist Gustad Noble who is very hard working and shown as a family man who is completely dedicate towards his family. He lives in Khodadad building with his wife Dilnivaz and three children Sohrab, Darius, and Roshan. He has two trustworthy friends, Dinshawji and Jimmy Bilmoria. Throughout his whole life learns several lessons of life in the novel.

Mistry has set the novel, *Such a Long Journey* against the background of the post- independent India and depicts the middle-class Parsee community of Khodadad building of Bombay during the period of 1960 and 1970. Though Mistry has been living in Canada for around 23 years but his memories and knowledge about Indian history is fresh. He uses history tremendously in his works and depicts the background of Indo–Pak war of 1971, that mainly deals with the colonial rule which led to birth of a new country as Bangladesh. We can read *Such a Long Journey* with two dimensions one is the frame of a novels portray showing the war history and another is how Mistry expresses the life of Khodadad inhabitants getting affected because of different incidents. He throws light on political issues and corruption prevailing in the country.

Rohinton Mistry expresses how the war leaves a harsh impact on an individual's life. The war of Indo-Pak which happened in 1971 was sparked off by the general elections of Pakistan. In August 1947, the partition of India at the time of independence had given birth to two nations India and Pakistan. Pakistan was made up of two geographically divided areas in east and west of India. The two parts of Pakistan were named as West Pakistan and East Pakistan. Later East Pakistan was converted into Bangladesh. The population, political and economic power were similar but West Pakistan achieved a dominant position in **'Pakistan's**

army against East Pakistan'. This left an impact on the Bengali leader of East Pakistan, Sheikh Mujibur Rehman who decided to make opposition political party known as Awami League and demanded more rights and freedom for East Pakistan.

General Yahya Khan, the military dictator of Pakistan held a general election in December 1970. In this election, the Awami League leader Sheikh Rehman won 99 percent seats in East Bengal and an overall majority in Pakistan's National Assembly. Zulfikar Ali Bhutto the leading politician of West Pakistan played a game and refused to let Awami Party make a government. He put Sheikh Rehman behind bars. West Pakistan dominated East Pakistan very badly that time. They imposed a merciless game of terror by killing innocent citizens. For over six months, they continued the heinous crimes like rape, torture, murder of innocent East Pakistanis which finally led to migration of more than 7 million refugees to the neighboring country, India.

The Awami League leaders somehow became successful in escaping to Calcutta and form a government of Bangladesh in exile. This government was constituted by the Mukti Bahini which had expressed its significance by the name 'Liberation Army' and launched a movement of guerrilla warfare. On 27th March 1971, the Indian Prime Minister Indira Gandhi expressed full support for East Pakistan and its leaders who were struggling for freedom. Indian leadership and East Pakistan army officers made a strategy to end the genocide by taking armed actions against Pakistan. They started establishing training camps and recruitment for Mukti Bahini guerrillas. Later, Mukti Bahini joined the Indian Army under the leadership of Indian Army General J.S. Arora. He moved forward within East Pakistan and after eleven days of fight they surrounded the Pakistani garrison. On 16 December 1971, they defeated the ninety-three thousand strong Pakistani army and made it surrender. Eventually, East Pakistan won victory with the help and support from India and India played the role of a genuine and true friend with them. Owing to this act, India was praised by many countries. It has been an Indian culture to help others. This incidence of history developed a commitment to socialism and democracy.

Mistry also portrays other historical and political upheavals in the novel like Pak aggression on Kashmir, Indo-China war which happened in 1962 and the Indo-Pak war. He uses history as a base in his novel and depicts the common people's life through history. His characters are the mouthpieces of history who convey different incidents from the pages of history intertwined with their lives. Thus, the novel is a mixture of history and personal life of characters. This is a major plot in the novel and author relates it with his characters. Mistry uses the character of Major Jimmy Bilimoria who expresses history as his life goes around the Pro–Bangladesh war of 1971. His story is based on

Nagarwala conspiracy of 1971. He composites the character of Sohrab Nagarwala, a member of RAW and close person to Mrs. Indira Gandhi. RAW (***Research and Analysis Wing***) is the intelligence agency of India which was established in 1968. The works of this agency are to investigate and collect the international and national facts but the connotation of this term has been different in the novel. Prime Minister uses the agency for his dirty works.

Nagarwala had involvement in a scam of Rs 60 Lakh. He was arrested because he followed orders of Indira Gandhi. This money was planned to be sent to the fighters of Bangladesh. Bilimoria explains this whole incident to Gustad. After hearing all this his faith shatters. He says, ***"Everyone knows there is corruption. But on this level? Hard to believe" (SLJ,280).*** Bilimoria said that his crime was that he followed instructions of Mrs. Gandhi. Later he realizes that no money was received by Mukti Bahini and all money got transferred to the account of Mrs. Gandhi. Major said that people are talking about it and they are assuming that the money might be used for elections and his son's car business. This is actually true that all organizations and agencies are initially constituted with better perspectives, but politics is the key which makes everything dirty. Politicians always manipulate system for their own benefits only. After some months, Nagarwala was found dead in a mysterious condition. The death of Nagarwala changes many expressions of Parsee community. Through this incident, Mistry gets enlightened about how personal issues become political.

Moreover, Gustad as central figure of the novel also depicts how corruption and politics fill his and his family's lives with problems. War of Bangladesh is the best-suited example showing this because at that time war was like a contagious disease giving birth to millions of refugees. If it hadn't had happened, there was no need to collect funds for Mukti Bahini. War was the real culprit for his problems. Major Bilimoria was closely linked with the war and he had sent Rs 10 Lakh to Gustad. Hiding such an amount is not a child's game for middle class. Gustad was mere a bank clerk what reason he could give if someone detects the amount. He told Dinshawji that Bilimoria was working for a national cause and now all three of them were automatically associated with national affairs of India's involvement with Bangladesh. They all represented the ethnic Parsee community. So, this incident explains how directly and indirectly everyone was getting involved in corruption and politics.

The death of Lal Bahadur Shastri is also a national affair which makes situations worse. When the nation was filling up with the dirt of politics and corruption, many innocent legends died and Shastri was one of them. He was born in October 1904 and died in January 1966. He was an active leader of Congress party of India. He played a big role in Indian Independence Movement and his very famous slogan ***"Jai Jawan, Jai Kisan"*** had given positive vibes to the farmers. We can say he was a hero for them. Shastri was influenced by both Mahatma Gandhi and Jawaharlal Nehru and continued Nehruvian policies of socialism and non-alignment. He died of heart attack on 10 January 1966 at the time of Tashkent Agreement but no one was ready to believe this. Many assumptions were made in public however it was arguably said that his death was a murder. Everyone was impressed by his kind and generous behavior. On this, Dr. Paymaster said:

> Shastri died on Soviet soil, less than eighteenth months after he become Prime Minister. Some said he had been killed by the Pakistanis, and other suspected a Russian plot. Some even claimed it was the new Prime Minister's supporters who poisoned Shastri so that her father's dynastic–democratic dream could finally come true. (*SLJ*,114)

The above lines imply only one question which shook everyone's mind, who is actually the murderer, who is responsible for this? Mistry depicts Nehru's humiliation in the Indo-China war in 1962 and Shastri's becoming Prime Minister of India after death of Nehru. Mistry enlightens this scene by saying, the year of Indo-China war was a nightmare for the nation. It was very violent time for the nation, many buses were burned, curfew and lathi charge happened and this is a real picture of war. When it happens, many innocents die just because of personal grudges.

These were the major incidents of the novel, which depict the historical and political issues but we have some other incidents too. The author also depicts the politics and corruption on the grounds of majority and minority classes of the society. First, when Gustad reveals his nervousness for the people of his community thus, "no future for minorities with all these fascist Shiv Sena politics and Marathi language nonsense. It was going to be like the black people in America – twice as good as the Whiteman to get half as much". This is the majority and minority aspect of diaspora. Government is made for public help and they always give discourses on banishing the caste system and discrimination of color. They have been saying this in their speeches for many years that everyone is equal and liberal. But in reality, since ancient times all are not treated equal. In today's time, majority dominates minority and Gustad faces the same fate in the story. Second, when Mrs. Indira Gandhi "nationalized the banks, it destroyed the sovereignty of Parsees over the banking system". When Dinshawji informs Gustad about Gandhi's decision to nationalize the banks, he feels disheartened because Parsees were the kings of banking in those days. He had a good faith on government, but his faith was shattering day by day. He shares his views with his wife and his friend Dinshawji that this is a political strategy of Mrs. Gandhi to get interest from Parsee bankers and nationalization of banks would not work well. Parsees felt insecure in Mumbai. Dinshawji says to his friend, ***"Wait till the Marathas take over, then we will have real Gandoo Raj" (SLJ,6).***

Another point highlighting corruption in politics was the incident of death of Feroze Jehangir Gandhi who was also Parsee. He was born in September 1912 and died in September 1960. He was a politician and journalist. He got married to Indira Gandhi in 1942 and become a member of Nehru–Gandhian family. In his political career, he became the Member of Parliament in 1950. In the novel, Mistry relates his death with Khodadad inhabitants and Dilnivaz says on demise of Feroze Gandhi that he was never liked by Nehru from the beginning, Dinshawji agrees with her words: ***'That was tragic Even today, people say Ferozes heart attack was not really a heart attack'(SLJ,7).***

Parsee individuals like Dilnivaz and Dinshawji are shown to be trying to look at different facets of the so-called natural death of a member of their community. By above lines, Mistry implies Nehru's frustration and political image because he was obsessed with her "Darling Daughter Indira" who had left her husband and was living with her father. Here history leaves many questions to readers like why Shastri and Feroze both died with the heart attack? Is this true that they both had natural death or were both of them murdered? Were they poisoned? This is a naked dance of politics.

Furthermore, in *Such a Long Journey*, Mistry also depicts the loss of identity on historical grounds which is evident from scene talking about the issue of changing names of streets and places. When Dilniwaz comes to know about it, she says why the names were changed. They think that changing the names of streets and roads would be changing their identity. Names are essential part of one's identity in one's life. In my childhood, it was Lamington Road. It has vanished and is known by another name, Dadasaheb Bhadkhamkar Marg. Dilnivaz says with these names we have grown up and many of our memories are associated with them. On this David Williams said:

> Loss of old names is precisely the loss of the old logo-centric security, that metaphysical reassurance via language.... Ultimately, he experiences rewriting the map of his neighbourhood as an interruption in his self-presence (*Williams,* 271).

It implies here that if someone loses his/ her name, he or she doesn't only lose his/ her name but also his/ her identity. Name is something by which we can recognize and if someone takes it away from us then nothing remains. This is a part of alienation, nostalgia and loss of identity.

Mistry not only discusses politics and history, but he also shows the characters' struggle for hope and resettlement. Every person has many dreams in their lives and they have to go through many fights and hardships to achieve them. Gustad is one of them, whose dreams are modest and he wants to fulfill them. Mistry shares with us when Sohrab refuses to join IIT on Roshan's ninth birthday. Due to his such violent behaviour, Gustad's dreams and expectations are shattered for his son's future prosperity. He makes many efforts to guide him but Sohrab reacts violently and shouts:

> "I'm sick and tired of IIT, IIT, IIT all the time. I'm not interested in it, I'm not a jolly good fellow about it, and I'm not going there" (*SLJ*,10).

Gustad wanted to make his son a competent engineer. He says to Sohrab, I am a normal human being. I want to give my family a good and peaceful life. I have so many yearnings to you and don't want to save money. I buy almonds to make your mind sharp and you know we all are taking breathe in poisonous political air. This government can only gift us unemployment. He gives lessons to make up his mind, by stating that the time is so frustrating. He proposes that we should have just two decisions: one is socialism and other is a military autocracy. He gives a comment to forget democracy for a few years because it does not mean that we are starving for a country. He says that the ugliness, filth and miserable conditions of the city are just the epitome of what happens at the center. He tells all people involved in government are greedy creatures, disloyal and not trustworthy. They are fraud and corrupt and the entire situation will only be changing when the government will change. Every government only thinks about their own benefits and they never fulfill their promises.

Mistry presents two different dimensions of generations in *Such a Long Journey.* The protagonist Gustad and his friend Dinshawji come under the older generation who have some trust left in the ruling party to improve country's future. In younger generation come Sohrab and his friend. They demand something new in the nation. Between these two generations, Mistry's has shown some characters who have different dimensions for politics and history. Dr. Paymaster's adapt views about contemporary politics and Miss Kutpitia's and Dilnivaz's ignorance of the political changes are example of this.

Such a Long Journey has entwined the threads of history and social life in the novel. Through the characters like Gustad, Dinshawji, Dilnivaz, Bilimoria, the author portrays a good picture of Parsee community and their condition. We can say that the novel is a social document. Ultimately, *Such a Long Journey* is not only the expression and feelings of the author but it is also an account of Parsee community and moreover, it is an outcome and a tool to regain the loss of dignity, identity, self-respect and grace which the Parsees have lost. Mistry raises a strong and high-pitch voice for his community by his works. He also indicates every single person of his community. He raises many questionnaires in the novel when he demands equality.

A Fine Balance is set in mid-1970s and the book opens with a prologue of 1975, period of internal emergency imposed by Indira Gandhi and concludes with an epilogue of 1984, a period of death of Indira Gandhi by her Sikh bodyguards. The structure of the plot is simple and the novel consists of 614 pages, describing social and historical upheavals. All novels *Such a Long Journey* and *A Fine Balance,* and *Tales from Ferozsha Baag* can be judged with three common themes social, political and historical. They started from Such *a Long Journey* and comes to *A Fine Balance.* He also showcases the political issues of Indira Gandhi in his novel. In sixteen chapters of the novel, the author explains four main characters and their lives over a period of ten years. The novel also depicts the life and characters of Bombay, the City of Sea. The novel primarily concerns about the story of four unlikely characters that come together after the Government declares Internal State Emergency and eventually come together under one flag.

A Fine Balance is mainly made up of three narratives shown in the stories of four main characters, Dina, Ishwar, Om and Maneck. Mistry narrates the past lives of the major characters in first, third and fifth chapters. Rest of the chapters describe the period of time between the Prologue and Epilogue. Mistry's narratives move between the past and present smoothly with the characters living in India and contrasting with hopes of India's independence to form a corruption free society. Moreover, *A Fine Balance* has some similarities in beginning and end. First, the novel starts with stoppage of train with someone committing a suicide and ends too with train stoppage with someone committing a suicide. Second, it starts with the history and riots of 1947 and ends with 1984 Sikh riots. During this period, Sikhs got their hairs and beard cut to hide their identity. As T. Vijay Kumar comments: ***"A Fine Balance is a very saddening novel"***. It is sad because it shows a picture of shattered dreams of people to the readers.

A Fine Balance expresses his readers the heroic struggle of his four strong characters Dina Dalal, a beautiful widow in her forties, tailor Ishwar, Omprakash and Maneck Kolah, a young student. They are living the life which is full of pain, no one could have foreseen. The oppression and corruption are their main enemy in the novel and these two are the terms in which hardship and efforts are always denied by the oppressor. Ishwar and Omprakash have come to the Bombay city to earn a living but they are oppressed on many situations. At last, they start to earn in Dina's house. Though all four of them want to live a simple life, their yearnings and aspirations are modest but still they struggled. *A Fine Balance* starts with a very cynical tone of Maneck, who comes to study in Bombay and he starts living with Dina Dalal as a paying guest. Omprakash and Ishwar belong to Chamar caste they come from village as refugees in Bombay due to caste violence. They start working in Dina's house as tailors. All four belong to different caste and community but from this point they all start interacting with each other and get inter-linked. All four have come with an urge of better life. Dina wanted an independent life so she starts living alone after his husband's death. Maneck leaves his comfort at home and comes to fast city Bombay for further education and since Omprakash and Ishwar were dominated and oppressed by the upper caste people in their village so they migrate to Bombay for earnings and learn tailoring.

Mistry portrays the condition of four major characters well at the time of emergency. When Ishwar asks Dinabai, "I heard from someone about Emergency, what is that?". Then Dina replies that it is a sort of game for political powerful people and it doesn't affect ordinary people. Here Dina lied because she doesn't want to lose her paying guests. An emergency is like a disease for a nation which eats very slowly and only affects common people's life. Curfew, murder, rape, arrest, punishment and torture are only made for ordinary peoples and it is performed by the powerful and rich people. Through all these Mistry is depicting the scenario of political upheavals.

A Fine Balance actually shows the real picture at the time of independence and post–independence. At the time of Emergency, government implements MISA that means police has full rights to take anyone in custody, with fault and without fault. Under this act, Nawaz, the tailor is arrested by them on the charge of smuggling gold from the gulf. In fact, the poor tailor only asked for payment from the customer. Police mercilessly beats him and gives third degree. The normal people were not able to take a single breath of relief at the time of emergency and yes, this was the time, when white could be made black. After this incident, public lost all their faith in the government. The hoardings are thrashed and fired. The public become violent and they react. The Prime Minister gives the message that she is a servant, and will help the common people. If she is our servant, so where is she now? This is totally correct public elect government for them, but politicians never think about them. The politicians make false promises at the time of elections and forget afterwards. They make many schemes, but taxes take double from the people.

Mistry has divided the novel between the village and city. He shows us the picture how corruption affected both the communities at that time. In the village Thakur Dharamasi is the person who played the role of oppressor. He always dominated over the lower caste people and Narayan and his family were his main victim. During the election time, Narayan wants to cast his vote to his own caste (Chamar) candidate but he is kidnapped and tortured by the goons of Thakur. Here Mistry enlightens a very sensitive issue of Dalit consciousness which is still unresolved in the 21st century. In this text, the character of Thakur always wants supremacy on the lower strata of society.

Mistry not only highlights the emergency issue, in fact, he shares a vast image of it with the readers. At the time of emergency, many merciless acts have been performed which were just heinous crime. First, overpopulation is dealt at the time of emergency in an unprecedented way. Gandhi's son Sanjay Gandhi started a family planning program which is scientifically called vasectomy. This law was also passed by Mrs. Indira Gandhi and under this law, people are taken forcefully for operation. Even they who are bachelor or who are going to be married, they all were forced to undergo the operation. This was a cruel and inhuman act which happened during the emergency. Mrs. Gandhi passes another act according to which they who are dying during the emergency, their deaths will count accidental. This presents such a harsh picture of government.

Second, government makes false promises. They did many promises to poor and uneducated peoples but never fulfilled them. A number of speeches had been given during the election time by Mrs. Indira Gandhi.

> "We will open new schools, provide clean water and health care; promises of land and landless peasants, promises of powerful laws to punish any discrimination against, and harassment of, backward caste by upper caste; promises to abolish bondage labour, child laour, Sati, dowry system, child marriage" (*AFB,* 38).

The above lines signify that Mrs. Gandhi promised to do best for the public like opening schools, providing clean water, medical attentions, land agreements etc. but she did not give anything to them. Moreover, she gave torture, rape, curfew and much more. Later Indira Gandhi was found guilty. Dina raised her voice to say that after a charge of guilty, her enthusiasm is same like before, which means her attitude was just like before. She was not feeling guilty of what she did. She has not a single expression of sorry on her lips. Moreover, public asked many questions about this like why she was not charged, why she was not put in the jail. But there was no answer; nothing happened. She remains the same. After this, common public wanted to follow the path of freedom fighter Jaya Prakash Narayan. He was born in October 1902 and died in October 1979. He was an Indian activist who completely opposed Mrs. Indira Gandhi in 1970s. Many students felt if they follow Jaya Prakash Narayan, then radical reform would come. But student like Avinash looks the situation from different perspective. Seeing at the other side of coin, he says to Maneck:

> Three weeks ago, the High Court found the Prime Minister guilty of cheating in the last elections which meant she had to step down, but she began stalling. So, the opposite parties' student organizations, trade unions started mass demonstrations across the country all calling for her resignation. Then the government declared a State of Emergency (*AFB,* 245).

The above lines imply this is all political game which is not easily understandable by normal people. Avinash says we all are weak humans; we can't do anything. Emergency has strong reasons beyond our thoughts and approach. She is the lady who plays very well and we cannot do anything about it. All four main characters in *A Fine Balance* become victim of politics and oppression. Their stories overlap with those of each other. All fours have different lives and tasks in the novel. Dina, the female protagonist struggling for liberty represents a women plight in society. Maneck and Dina are Parsees, so they come under the periphery. Nusswan, brother of Dina Dalal, is a character who shows male dominance and patriarchy. He always uses old discourse on his sister after death of her husband. In earlier times a widow has to be *sati* with her husband at the time of his funeral.

Dina Dalal is a strong and liberal character. But on other hand, if we compare her with female characters of *Such a Long Journey,* Dilnivaz and Roshan, she is not like them. She is the woman who has the qualities of liberal and radical mind and wants freedom after her father's death. She has to accept Nusswan as her guardian but doesn't want to lose her liberty. She makes her different dimensions on marriages. She never says yes to any boy suggested by her brother. She marries a boy of her own choice, Rustom. She faces lots of problem after death of Rustom in an accident. She refuses to live with her brother. She lives alone and independently in her husband's flat. For many years she struggles and becomes helpless at the time of eviction from her flat. Since no place is left for him to live, so she goes to her brother's home.

Here from the feminist perspective, Mistry does injustice with her. From the beginning of the novel, he expresses her to be strong, liberal and independent but towards the end she too has to go under patriarchy. If we compare the women characters of *Such a Long Journey* and *A Fine Balance,* we can see that they are different with each other. Dilnivaz and Roshan are not as liberal-minded women like Dina Dalal.

On this, Mistry has also given a feminist point of view in the novel. Critical thinker, N. Kavitha in her paper "A critical study of women in *A Fine Balance*" also attempts this. But my perspective is different and new. I would like to say here that this has not only happened in earlier times, but it also happens in the 21st century. Women are coming forward with education, career and they are becoming engineers, doctors, pilots and astronauts but they are still facing compulsions of patriarchy. Situation in metro cities is improving but the rural areas are still like before. After this incident many questions come in mind of the readers like whether Mistry is also an anti- feminist, whether Mistry too wants her female characters docile and submissive.

Thus, Mistry has his own way to show the situations at the time of emergency. He has given different dimensions to the reader and has added political–historical world in the novel. The omniscient narrator is the main point in the novel. By the epigraph we can easily feel the feelings of author:

> "Holding this book in your hand, sinking back in your soft armchair, you will say to yourself: perhaps it will amuse me. And after you read this story of great misfortunes, you will no doubt dine well, blaming the author for your own insensitivity, accusing him of wild exaggeration and flights of fancy, but rest assured; this tragedy is not a fiction. All is true." (***AFB***, Epigraph).

By this Mistry enlightens the issue of marginalized people and raises many questions. If we see our society, there are many marginalized communities – the Parsees, the Chamars, the Muslims, the Madaris, the beggars etc. They share same novelist group and history and many critics have been continually writing on them, but years pass and nothing changes. All four characters in *A Fine Balance* have no control over their circumstances. History makes them history, Om and Ishwar belong to the Chamar caste. Misrty makes a kaleidoscopic image of modern Indian society by his characters Dukhi, Roopa, Radha, Om, Ishwar, and Narayan. They all come under the subalterns. In the novel, they are both oppressor and oppressed. The incident when a Bhangi comes to hut of Narayan, her wife Roopa shouts at him. She thinks that they are Chamar and he is Bhangi. So, he is not equal to them. This is the common mentality of people which is a big hurdle for equality.

At last, *A Fine Balance* novel has ended with anti-Sikh riots in Delhi. Indira Gandhi's death resulted in riots and killing of many innocent people. In the last scene, the taxi driver advises Maneck to cut off his beard because that time Sikhs people were being butchered and cut like vegetables. He says that she (Mrs Gandhi) blessed us with bombs and guns. Actually, every government thinks of their profit only. They never think what impact their small and big decisions may leave on ordinary people. Many critics have made a comparison between *A Fine Balance* and Salman Rushdie's *Midnight Children*. Both the novels are set in Bombay and both have a backdrop of emergency. On the other hand, they are quite different to each other. One is concerned with Muslim middle class while other is related to Parsee and lower strata of the society.

Subsequently, all of Mistry's works play within the frame lines of the private and the public. Most of his main protagonists and central figures such as Gustad Noble and Dina are the two realms and they are depicted judging the boundaries of both. The public world is the world of the ordinary citizen, consisting of friends, acquaintances and the professional space of work where adult relationships are made day by day. In the meantime, we are indicated towards the themes of politics, history and historical figures and community which are an integral part of the lives of Mistry's characters. The private world is the space of home and homelands and the family blood relations. This mostly constitutes women and children, husbands and wives along with many other and meaningful relationships. Age is the central theme in Mistry's fiction and relationship between and across generations is a major concern whenever Mistry discusses the private realm of the family and the household. The private world is where the family gathers. In Mistry's fiction, it consists of the world of the old and the young. Women dominate the private realm with their nurturing attention and the hard labor through which the stability of the family is ensured.

We can say that the middle class and working class meet and greet and sympathize with each other, and learn to overcome their prejudices, values bonds of friendship, benevolence affection and humanity. In many interviews, Mistry has stated that this novel started with the image of a woman at a sewing machine- and was later expanded to include the tailors. It means it is a journey tale of ordinary women to become a tailor. It is also to bring in the horror of caste problems and violence of rural India, and the figure of Maneck Kohlah from Kashmir. All these characters, together with Dina are portrayed as fiery-tempered, intelligent, fiercely independent, aged woman. It is a small world of recreated family of the novel. Mistry's fiction has moved from the family in *Tales from Ferozshah Baag* to the wider range of Parsees community in his work, *Such a Long Journey*. *A Fine Balance* again moves back to the theme of the family and relations and uses many narrative strategies to make the beautiful plot. Through this human interest and the sense that the characters are firmly enabled in their present works, he makes the plot. Rohinton presents new diasporas which acknowledge the adjustments in their Indian culture and advances with it.

Therefore, *Such a Long Journey* and *A Fine Balance* manage subjects like the quest for identity, self –

centered immigrant psyche, the conflict between homes, a critique of power and politics, journey, history, nostalgia, relationships, movement, multiculturalism, religion, social angles, monetary imbalance, fundamentalism and terrorist savagery. These issues are not new but they are more significant than any time in recent memory in the dynamic image of the world today.

Such a Long Journey and *A Fine Balance* both the novels are the masterpieces of Rohinton Mistry. If we talk about *Such a Long Journey,* the journey word mainly signifies Gustad's character because from the beginning till the end of the novel, he suffers a lot. Mistry shows how his life deals with hurdles. His life goes with lots of up and down but after all this, he always takes the next step to come forward in life. Nothing is balanced in the novel, *A Fine Balance.* We should say this novel is an epic of the suffering of human lives. All four characters continue to fight till the end. All four have the same yearnings and dreams like Gustad and they also face the real hardships of social, political and historical disturbances. Their lives are a total imbalance.

Tales from Firozsha Baag Mistry describes the ethnic conflict faced by the Parsees from the right-wing political parties in the city of Bombay such as the Shiv Sena. In the process they face a loss of their social, economic as well as political standing. The characters face all kinds of ethnic conflicts with the communities that claim to be the 'sons of the soil'.

The Parsees, during the pre-colonial era did not have any significant influence on Indian society. With the arrival of the British and subsequent increase of the Parsee influence redefined their role and identity. They soon became the richest community in India and were quick to adopt the English life style. In the post-colonial era witnessed the decline of the community in terms of population and impact. Ethnic conflicts are considered as the overriding reason for this decline. Mistry's writings take into account the pessimism prevailing within the community as well as the loss of influence and power over the Indian society. His writings also extend to the contemporary ethnic conflicts faced by the community. As a response, the community members have gradually withdrawn their participation from the larger cultural, and socio-economic activities.

Tales from Firozsha Baag engages with the issue of the ethnic identity of the Parsees in the post-independence India. The stories are based on the experiences of the residents of a Parsee dominated residential complex that suggests a ghettoed existence. The vivid description of this housing complex suggests that it came up as a response to the external threats.

The residents of the housing complex display various shades of Parsee life in the newly independent state of India. Mistry describes the traditional side of Parsee life with all the rites, beliefs and other cultural practices. The author explores the withdrawal of the Parsees from the social, economic and political settings as a direct response to the hostility they face from external agents. The humiliation and violence faced by the residents as described in the novel has confined them to this ghettoed existence.

In *Auspicious Occasion,* Rustomji, an educated lawyer faces a humiliating situation when someone spits paan juice on him on the auspicious day of the Parsee New Year. He starts name calling those around him and uses the term, ghatis which means uncivilized. He aggravates the mob and then plays the clown to save himself. The Parsees reconstructed their racial identity as a different race in an attempt to separate themselves from the rest of the population. They mostly considered themselves equal in rank to the British. They established themselves as an influential community during the colonial rule. Despite their past impact and power, Mistry presents a curious case of the community that built the city of Bombay is now getting ridiculed by the ghatis. The outside seems to have structured itself politically and economically along with strong social ties, while the Parsees slip into both, external and internal conflicts.

In the story, *Collectors,* Mistry presents a case of a riot organized by the right wingers and suggests that the Parsees were forced into ethnic conflicts. There is also an attempt by Mistry to compare the sufferings of the marginalized communities with those of the Parsees. Mistry attempts to interlink these sufferings to shed light on the rampant corruption and lack of social justice in the country. In his short story, *Paying Guests,* a character named Boman states, "There are laws to protect the poor, Boman said bitterly after he got home, and laws to protect the rich. But middle-class people like us get the bamboo, all the way".

The characters in the stories reflect Mistry's own pessimistic attitude toward India. With the increasing politically charged conflicts and marginalization of the residents, the characters can only see it as a land of hopelessness. They seek to move to other prosperous nations to start anew.

In the final story, *Swimming Lessons,* Mistry again draws attention to the political nature of various ethnic clashes. He is critical of Shiv Sena's leaders and their actions in Maharashtra. The author believes that the party often leads the clashes. The protagonist's mother states, "Shiv Sena agitation about Maharashtra for Maharashtrians, threatening strikes and Bombay bundh all the time, with no respect for the public".

Mistry presents negative side of Bombay, as a city painted with violent colors. Mistry projects himself as a realist who has lived long enough in Bombay to write about a true Parsee experience in the city and there is no illusion that he wants to entertain in his fiction. He knows the pulse of the city that he describes because he has lived long in Bombay. For the author, it is the ones in power that are responsible for such deeply disturbing experiences of alienation and marginalization. These experiences are carried by the members of the community for a lifetime as they develop an inherent pessimistic attitude. Wherever they go they suffer from the anxieties pertaining to rejection and violent conflicts.

Eventually, *Such a Long Journey, A Fine Balance* and *Tales from Firozsha Baag* portray the microcosm of life in general and political disturbances in particular, which Mistry experienced when he was in India. His experiences of migration lead him to compare India with Canada. He is a multi-cultural person, but nation's blood flows in his veins. Rohinton Mistry through his writing wants that one person should understand another. India is a country of laws and regulations, and we should obey them. We should respect every caste and community. We should live and let others live with peace and harmony. We should genuinely follow the concept of equality and freedom.

Chapter Three

Critical Analysis of Community and Caste Imbalances of India in Rohinton Mistry Context

India is a multicultural country and we can feel fragrance of different religions and cultures here. There are four major religions prevailing as we all known through our history: Hinduism, Islam, Sikhism and Christianity. We also have other religions practiced and followed by different communities. Some of the common religions are Jainism, Buddhism and Judaism. These religions are further divided into various categories and sub-categories of caste, class and community.

Community is a social unit that shares common values and a group of people who are connected by a relation. On the other hand, caste is a social system which grades the society. There are many theories behind existence of caste system in India which can be said to be ***"religious and biological"***. With the perspective of religious theory, classification of Indian caste is based on *varnas*.

The varna system divides the society into four classes on the basis of their ranks, occupation, power and privilege. According to the religious text, ManuSmriti has divided the Hindu world in castes and sub-castes. ManuSmriti is an ancient prominent legal book in DharamShastra of Hinduism. It divides Hindus into four varnas: Brahmin, Kshatriya, Vaishya and Shudra. Manu hadn't just divided them in upper, middle and lower classes but had also tagged them with different names establishing supremacy of upper over lower strata of society. Further, he also proposes *gotra, sub- gotra, pind* and *sub – pind.*

Manu had compared these four divisions with parts of human body showing their respective position in the society. First, Brahmins are blessed by the mouth of the body. He mentions in his Dharma Shastra book that Brahmins have full rights to read Vedas and can give discourses on this to people of society. He tags them with the name of upper- caste and assigns them the occupation of priests and teachers. Second come Kshatriyas who are supposed to be the shoulders of the body. Manu has given them the right to learn the Vedas but they can't teach it to anyone. According to him, they are upper–middle class and they can be soldiers or fighters by their occupation. Third we have Vaishyas they represent the thigh of the body and Manu says in his book that there is no need for them to read, learn and teach the Vedas. They can choose their occupation as businessmen. Last category is Shudras, the untouchables. Yes, people identify this class by this word. Manu had linked them with the foot of the body. They don't have any right to touch Veda's text. They can't even touch the people of upper caste. According to him, they are the servant of all three castes and he suggested in his book that if they want to apologize for any of their faults, they should serve Kshatriyas. On the other hand, he comments, if they want to go to heaven, they must follow all the orders of Brahmins.

The concept of biological theory about the varnas is different. It compares the system with three qualities (*gunas*) like *Sattva, Rajas* and *Tamas* and they all have different shades. Sattva is white, Rajas is red and Tamas is black. This theory divided them with the perspective quality. First, Sattva qualities expresses wisdom, pride, honour, truth and positivity. It is dedicated to the Brahmins. Second, Raja's qualities express strength and intelligence and are dedicated to Kshatriyas and Vaishyas. Third and last, Tamas qualities express dullness, stupidity, idiocy, lack of creativity and negative feelings and are completely dedicated to Shudras. This is so indigestible in today's era how our ancestors had created theories and categorized people on the basis of caste.

After independence in 1947, India got political freedom from the Britishers, but one community could not get their freedom till date and animals are better treated as compared to them. No one knows what their fault is. They have the same blood, skin and everything still they are recognized as untouchables means *'Achhoot'* in hindi. Shudra or untouchable is the community which is marginalized in their own nation and feels a situation of alienation around their own people. The famous classical Sanskrit scholar, Kalidas has written a verse showing the position of shudras in the society which means drums, Shudras and Women are born to be beaten. These words express that he was very harsh and insensitive about them. From the feminist perspective we can see that women are also not liked by him and they also don't have the freedom and liberty just like Shudras. To add more to the agony, Shudra women are doubly marginalized in society because one fault of theirs is that they have born in Shudra community and other is that she is a woman.

History has not only given us politics, corruption and war, but also caste system and capitalism. The human society is further divided into upper caste, middle caste and lower caste. In our Indian history, we have so many examples of domination of the lower caste and community. If we look at our society about two decades ago, name of a lady thrills our body. She was Phulan Devi who belonged to lower caste and her full life was oppressed by Thakurs, the so-called upper caste of society. It would be difficult to say what her fault was. She was kidnapped, beaten and raped several times by many Thakurs. This heinous act of Thakurs raises many questions. Though people from lower caste are not allowed to touch people of upper caste, but they can use them to fulfill their sexual pleasures. Such issues create an imbalance regarding the community and caste.

In Indian literature, there are many names who have highlighted the issues of caste differences, discrimination and subjugation in their writings. Mulk Raj Anand and Raja Rao are the two prominent authors who have penned many works on these topics. Their text ***'Untouchable'*** and ***'Kanthapura'*** got very famous at their times and still have a great impact on the readers. Subsequently, there are so many communities in India who are facing problems regarding their identity. Parsees is one of them and they are a very small ethnos – religious minority in India mostly living in west coast of the sub-continent, especially in Mumbai and adjoining areas. Although they are very little in number but they occupied a notable place in India's social, cultural and political history.

A Fine Balance has many contemporary issues and themes. War is the main theme of the novel and Mistry portrays how the war makes imbalances of caste and community in India. In the novel, the main characters lose their identity and respect from the beginning till the end and express their quest for identity. Mistry, through historical facts presents what had happened in the post-colonial India in 1947 and at the time of Internal Emergency by Prime Minister Indira Gandhi. In post-colonial period, Indian society underwent many changes which were significant for the nation building process. The two major incidents that happened post-independence were the partition of India and the Emergency from 1975 to 1977. Mistry explores how the personal lives of people got affected by all this and his characters belong to those communities, who are marginalized members of Indian society such as the lower castes, Parsees, Sikhs, Muslims and poor people. On this Peter Morey says: The inception of the Emergency was the result of an economic crisis which happened in the early 1970s. It can be said to be a result of emergence of Indira Gandhi as the national champion of the 1971 India–Pakistan war and her becoming a tyrant three and a half years later. Mrs. Indira Gandhi's political Emergency has created many imbalances in the narratives of nationhood.

Mistry presents a vast image of nation in his second novel and tells us the life of marginalized, the subaltern and the poor people in the nation. In the novel, the characters come from different social backgrounds and they are marginalized voices, but the characters of Om and Ishwar are the main victims of the caste system. The two characters are related to each other Ishvar is uncle and Om is son of Narayan. Both come to the city from their village to get some earning. They both become the main victim of the caste system because they are Chamar, the Dalit and untouchable by their caste. They start living in Dina's flat and through these characters, Mistry here expresses friendship, benevolence and relations. They all become a family unit by the impacts of political and social situation of nation. They are treated equal by Dina but their lives get imbalanced by the discomfort of Emergency. Lives of Ishvar and Om get worse by the government's family programme of sterilization. Dina also loses her flat and business and undergoes the patriarchy of her brother, Nusswan. Maneck the paying guest of Dina, commits suicide at the end of the novel. D'Cruz observes that ***"the political situation of the Emergency like an uncontainable and irrational force to frustrate the personal people's lives"*.**

In ancient times, upper caste never wanted the lower caste people to do the jobs and earn the bread by their own. Moreover, they identified Chamar as the people who worked with leather and their occupation included sweeping of toilets, carrying garbage of other people, shoe-making etc. They were often called by the name of *Choti Jaat*. The character of Dukhi, father of Ishwar and Narayan, dared to break the chain of caste system. Mistry says:

> Dukhi Mochi had two sons, Ishvar and Narayan and his decision to bring them into tailoring was indeed courageous, considering that the prime of his own life had been spent in

> obedient compliance with the traditions of the caste system. Like his forefathers before him, he had accepted from childhood the occupation preordained for his present incarnation. (*AFB*,18)

The above lines imply that Dukhi and his wife Roopa do not want their children to follow the rules of caste–based occupation. Ashraf, a Muslim tailor is a close friend of Dukhi mochi and he agrees to teach his children tailoring. They were happily welcomed in his home by him and his wife Mumtaz. Ishvar and Narayan learned tailoring very well. Mistry narrating through these lines mentions how difficult it is to fight against the caste system in India.

The author shows how independence of India gave a wide canvas of partition and riots between Hindus and Muslims. Mistry's characters make their own strategies to handle all these riots and emergency. He gives a very good example of this by showing the incidence at Ashraf's shop. He belongs to Muslim minority group and his shop carries the name of Muzaffar Tailoring Company. But at the time of Hindu–Muslim riots he changes his shop's name to Krishna Tailors for the security of his family. Once a group of 20 people comes to his shop, as they got to know from somewhere that this is a shop of Muslim owner. The situation was aptly handled by Ishvar and Narayan who assure them that the shop is a hindu shop. Still for the confirmation, the mob forces them to drop their pajamas and check whether they are circumcised or not. Only after the leader gets satisfied seeing their skin intact, they leave the shop soon. Mumtaz touches their feet and says that she will always be thankful to both of them for saving their lives. When Dukhi hears about all these, he appreciates them. This act shows both the positive and negative sides of human nature. On one side, communities were imbalanced as Dukhi, despite being a hindu was ill-treated by his own community. On the other side, the incident expresses that love remains in their heart because both Dukhi and Ashraf belonged to different religions but communal imbalances were not able to break their emotional ties and relationship and friendship between these two characters is the best example of humanity. The nation was dealing with war with the neighboring country but on the other hand, people from different communities and castes were living like a family unit. Ashraf, Mumtaz and Om are the perfect examples showing this. On the contrary, Thakur is an example who oppresses people of his own religion. Mistry conveys a message that ideal relationship is above the barriers of caste, community and religion.

A Fine Balance not only deals with community imbalances but also depicts the scenario of caste differences. Narayan gets married to a beautiful girl named Radha and they have a son Omprakash. He learns tailoring in the company of Ishvar. When State Assembly Elections are announced, Narayan wants to cast his vote to a candidate of his own caste. Through this episode the author introduces the oppressor of the novel named Thakur Dharamsi. He is the man who is class – conscious and wants to make people of Chamar community his servants. When he learns that Narayan wants to give his vote in favor of a candidate of his choice, he gets furious. He orders his goons to kidnap Narayan and two more people who support him. All three captives are taken to the farms of Thakur where they are brutally beaten, hung naked on banyan tree, and mercilessly flogged by them. They torture them to the extreme and urinate on their faces. They play a naked dance of oppression and domination like animals. They fill their mouth and genitals with burning coals. Narayan and his accomplishes ask for help from other villagers but no one come forward in their support. Ultimately, their lips and tongue melt and then their bodies are taken down from the tree.

The moment they begin to stir, Thakur's men realize that they are still alive, so they take the ropes from their ankles and tie it to their necks. They are finally hanged to death and their dead bodies are displayed in the village to give a lesson to the villagers. Narayan and his friends die without having any fault and this is such a heinous crime. After this, the violence and domination get worse and when Thakur's men are free from the duties of elections, they once again start harassing untouchables. Mistry gives a harsh picture of Thakur Dharamsi here:

> They beat up individuals at random in the streets, stripped some women, raped others, and burned a few huts. News of the rampage soon spread. People hid, waiting for the storm to blow order over (*AFB*,19).

The above lines expressed how the goons of Thakur took advantage of emergency and played their dirty games. They beat up innocent peoples, tortured them and during the time of emergency many virgin girls lost their virginity because of rape. It is a bitter fact that emergency, riots and partition not only give rise to violence, curfews, harassment etc. but they also affect lives of common people physically and psychologically.

Thakur Dharamsi always thinks of taking revenge in his mind from poor Dukhi mochi as he sent his son, Ishvar and grandson to city for better life and did not choose shoe-making as an occupation for them. Thakur thinks that Dukhi has done a crime to cross the line of caste and this is a punishable act. By Narayan's death, he has given them the gift of punishment. This incident reaches the climax in the novel, when Dukhi, Roopa, Radha and their daughter are bound and dragged into the dark main room to see the dead body of Narayan. Mistry expresses extreme cruelty of Thakur Dharamsi and narrates:

> The light tore away the benevolent cloak of darkness. The naked corpse's face was a burnt and broken blur. Only by the red birthmark on his chest they recognized Narayan. A long howl broke from Radha. But the sound of grief soon mingled with the family's death agony; the house was set alight (*AFB*,20).

The above lines imply the scene of darkness. I want to give this situation a new name; this was the night of no moon for Dukhi and his family. The body was naked, lips burnt, many bones broken and private parts were cut and no one was able to identify without the birthmark of the chest. It was such an extreme level of the crime. It shows the inhuman character of Thakur how he can do all this. By this episode the author expresses that he has no heart.

Furthermore, Ishvar and Om are unaware of this incident but later when they hear in town that bodies are flown in the river, they go to Police Station to register an F.I.R. At the Police Station, both of them are disrespected by the police inspector. Obviously, who is going to take interest in death of ordinary people in a country like ours? They feel their rejection and betrayal. After repeated requests, inspector agrees to look into the matter. He goes to the house and confirms that no crime has happened there and warns them of the dire consequences if they bother him again. The sub–inspector says to Ishvar:

> What kind of rascality is this? Trying to fill up the F.I.R with lies? You achhot caste are always out to make trouble! Get out before we charge you with public mischief! (AFB,21).

The above lines imply that police too had not supported them. Police are the public servants but they also have a sense of *jaat – paat* (casteism). Their duty is to help the victims, but they often do not abide by their duties and responsibilities. They also torture, reject, insult and sometimes make fun of the downtrodden people of the society. They have to follow the constitution and legal law. But in *A Fine Balance,* the police are shown to be different and as a puppet in the hands of Thakur.

Ashraf and Mumtaz, good friends of Dukhi feel very bad for them and try to console them. They were unable to find words to console Om and Ishvar. Nobody dared to help them. Through these scenes, many questions arise like whether the untouchables are born for injustice only, or they are not human beings, whether they are born to become servants only, why all these happen. These are just questions which are not going to be answered ever because we humans create differences of caste and community and only, we are there who can prevent it.

Furthermore, Thakur Dharamsi not only oppresses Narayan, in fact Om, Narayan's child, also becomes a victim of Thakur at a political level. The sterilization programme was implemented by the government on the decision taken by Mrs. Indira Gandhi to control the population and advised by Sanjay Gandhi during the time of Emergency. Thakur was the person who looked after this family planning programme. Thakur misused this program and police helped him in his misconduct. One day Om and Ishvar go to the market. They see that police arrest people and leave them to the camps forcefully. Om and Ishvar also get arrested by the police. On the orders of Thakur, Om's testicles are removed and Ishvar's legs are cut off due to the unsterilized operation.

Ultimately, Dr says: ***"If we start believing you, then all the eunuchs in the country will come dancing to us, blaming us for their conditions, trying to get money out of us"*** (AFB, 540). The above lines express about imbalances towards the eunuch's community of the society. Mistry says that the existence of this community in the world is linked to their dance and entertainment of others only. According to Serena Nanda's description, Hijra or eunuch is the third gender. It is neither male nor female and may contain elements of both the genders. Om and Ishvar also become similar to this. Om is now impotent and chooses to be a beggar. This is actually a reality as it is well known that hundreds of children are kidnapped in a year and their hands or legs are chopped off brutally by their kidnappers. They become the beggars at last as they do not have any other option.

The author shows the domination of different person in different manner. Taking the example of Dina, there is no caste system but still, she is dominated by her own brother. Dina Dalal is a beautiful Parsee widow woman. Her father was a doctor and she was rich at her father's time. When her father dies in an accident, she lives with her brother and mother and, her brother Nusswan is a patriarchal figure in the home. On that, she suffers a lot during her teenage and also sexually exploited by him. He beats her several times badly and always calls her a "loose woman". In one of the scenes presented by Mistry, one day Nusswan take her away for a wash, and throws cold water on her. Shivering with cold, she starts staring at him and her nipples get stiff. Despite being a brother, Nusswan pinches one badly and says, ***"Look at your little breast, you think you are a woman"***. In Indian society elder brother is always considered to be like father, so how he can do all these shitty things with her. This shows his domination over Dina in her own house.

However, when she grows up to be a woman, he searches for a suitable match for her and finds many prospective grooms for her, but she never approves any. Dina being an independent and liberal girl chooses to marry Rustom on her own choice. Unfortunately, her husband also dies in an accident like her father. She does not want to be a burden on her brother so she chooses to live independently in her husband's flat. She starts her business of tailoring and finds Om and Ishvar as his helpers. Maneck also joins them and all four- start staying with each other.

Dina's character shows a picture of hope and despair and shows how Dina and all characters' lives revolve between these two aspects. Mr. Valmik suggests Dina Dalal, ***"There is always hope – hope enough to balance our despair. Or we would be lost"* (AFB, 22).** There are some other characters in the novel like Rajaram, hair- collector and beggar master who also play their important roles in the story. All characters play a role to make things balanced but nothing works. The nation and people around it full of corruption and violence. Mistry portrays the body in the novel with the examples of sterilization and caste – differences.

A Fine Balance is an absorbing book about the life of common people whose lives are caught by the poverty. The novel shows a broad picture of present-day India, shows the sufferings, pain and screams of lower caste people. Through this novel, Mistry raises an apt and burning question on which we all need to ponder. How can the people of lower caste survive on the earth of death? The poor are the main victim of the novel, the powerful people make them homeless, mutilated and poisoned. Actually, the author presents a world where nothing is going to change for poor and the lower strata of society. He says society is only for the rich, the corrupt and for the oppressors. Mistry says that miseries of lower caste people start from the beginning of their life and end with their death. No one is ready to cope with them or to have some mercy on them. He expresses his characters their feelings and emotions through their heroes. It is necessary that we should change our minds, then it may change.

Mistry's first novel, *Such a Long Journey,* has elements of Parsee minority. Religious minority is not a new thing in the society. It has been known from ancient times, but ethnic minorities did not become an issue in European politics until the rise of nationalism in the 19th century. The minority group makes their own culture as national identity and the Parsees have always been at the forefront ever since. They show their cultural space through their writings. We have a number of ethnic – religious writers who write about their own religion with their diasporic experiences, like Bapsi Sidhwa, Farrukh Dhondy, Firdaus Kanga, Rohinton Mistry, Boman Desai and Dina Mehta.

Such a Long journey can be studied at three different levels: the tale of sufferings and struggle of middle-class minority, a journey of Gustad Noble and political and historical disturbances in the nation. The novel has many characters, but the main character is Gustad Noble whose journey is linked with the theme of war. Gustad's grandfather was a well-established man. His grandfather was a lover of books, was a prosperous furniture dealer. His all fortunes were squandered by his alcoholic uncle, but his father was a gentleman and was a loyal person to his family. Gustad has always been nostalgic with his grandfather's images and memories and always wants to make a building of bookcase with his eldest son, Sohrab. Mistry presents a broad image of middle-class Parsees through inhabitants of Khodadad building. Gustad also expresses and interacts with the outside community of Khodadad building. One such character is Dinshawji, a bank associate and his friend and his nature is comical in the novel. Gustad has another friend, Malcolm Saldhana, who is a western musician at the Mount Mary Church. Some other characters include Dr. Pay Master; Dr. Lord; Peerbhoy Paanwala, who has varieties of Paan; the bank manager Mr. Madan; the office peon; photographer of Nixon and Kissinger for the toilet training of the children of jhopadpatti (slums).

The vague and irresolute lives are the result of character emergency and clashes looked by the diasporic individuals. Ordinarily when an individual takes on another world, (s)he is casualty of that obliviousness because of which (s)he turns into an auxiliary animal in an unfamiliar land. Exactly the same thing turns out in the instances of the Parsees in Parsee writing, "both the Parsees who looked for greener fields in the West and the individuals who remained all in India have encountered personality emergency and disarray". They battle to make their own space in the West just as in India and the indistinguishable struggle of being a Parsee and the individual from an outcast local area precedes their osmosis. As an outcome they free their desires, expectations and aspirations and become minimized in the two spots whether in India or in an unfamiliar land. The flourishing prevalence of the works of the edge in diasporic writing accentuation the way that character is the foremost hunt of a person. As an essayist of diaspora Rohinton Mistry likewise depicts this personality journey. He composes on the indistinguishable battle of the Parsees.

Rohinton Mistry, in *Such a Long Journey,* portrays the political scenario of the post – independent India during the decades of sixties and seventies. The novelist leaves us to do a debate on socio – political situation with the corruption. He also raises day to day issues of Parsees and interlinks it with personal and political scenarios.

Such a Long Journey, Mistry has a significance of the word 'Journey'. The word has different meanings like the journey of pain and sufferings of inhabitants of Khodadad building, journey of Gustad's struggle for a better life. Mistry cited a total of three epigraphs in the novel and all three have different meanings with that. First epigraph is cited by the epic Shahnameh. This is a long poetry-based great epic of Parsees, written by poet Firdausi. People recognize the poet by the name of Firdausi but his real name was Mansur Ben Hasan. He started writing the epic in 977 AD and completed on 8th march 1010. It contains 50,000 couplets, around 60,000 verses and is known as world's longest epic. This epic mainly gives the knowledge about the Persian customs, culture, myths and history. The epic shares a deep knowledge about Parsees. On history of Parsees, he wrote about the beginning of the religion with the death of the last ruler named Sassanid Persian during the Muslims' conquest and end of Zoroastrianism in Iran. The first epigraph by author mentions:

He assembled the aged priest and put questions to them concerning the kings who had once possessed the world.

> 'How did they,' he enquired, 'hold the world in the beginning, and why is it that it has been left to us in such a sorry state? And how was it that they were able to live free of care during the days of their heroic labours?" (Firdausi Shah – Nameh, 1010)

The above lines relate to the history of Parsees. It reflects the Iranian culture which was very popular before the Arab invasion in 639 A.D. This is so true that Parsee had *Such a Long Journey* to India from Persia. They were permitted to live in Gujrat, at the instruction of King of Sanjan named Jadav Rana. The Parsees used to call their priests as Dustur who performed certain duties as instructed by the king. With the help of Dusturji, King said that this is a glass of milk and I am adding sugar into it and you should mix like this in our nation. The Parsees mixed deeply which is evident form the fact that they are not easily traceable in many cities.

The second epigraph is quoted by Rohinton Mistry from the poetry of T.S Eliot, *A Journey of Magi*. This poem was written in 1927 and contains 43 lines. T.S Eliot got converted to Anglo–Catholicism in his early days. In his poem, he tells us the journey of Magi with a situation of alienation and powerlessness which means the journey of East toward Christ and Christianity. The other critics comment on it that Eliot expresses his own journey of searching a satisfaction in Christianity by the poem. Mistry said:

> A cold coming, we had of it,
>
> Just the worst time of the year
>
> For a journey, and Such a Long journey...
(T.S Eliot, 1)

The above lines imply that in Eliot's poetry, journey word has a different significance. Here poet expresses Magi is about the priestly class of magicians and Mistry expresses the journey of Parsees. Eliot connects the words like coming, worst time which reflect the journey of Magi. Here the word 'Journey' signifies the quest for the spiritual land and about the transformation of religion. By this quote, the author depicts the Zoroastrians' journey and its followers with their culture ethos. He also gives the knowledge of their pains and sufferings about their religion.

Third, he quotes the epigraph of Gitanjali written by Rabindranath Tagore. Rabindranath Tagore was a Bengali writer and is known by the name of Rabi. He was born in 1817 and died in 1905. He has received Noble prize and many other prizes for his works. He wrote many works and Gitanjali is one of them. Gitanjali is a collection of 157 poems in Bengali version but in English version it has only 103 poems. It was published on 14 August 1910 and was translated in many other languages. It is very famous in the East in its English Version. Thus, Mistry uses:

> When old words die out of the tongue, new
>
> Melodies break forth from the heart, and were the
>
> ***Old tracks are lost, new country is reverted with its wonders. (Gitanjali, 132)***

The above lines imply migration of Parsees community from one place to another. He says that was the situation when they were getting nostalgic for their languages and places. He says that when a person leaves his roots then his heart gets filled with the memories of past. The title of the poem is very symbolic here because the word *Geet* means song here and *Anjali* means offering.

So, the meaning of this quote portrays melodies of the alienated and dispersed people.

Such a Long Journey is set on the backdrop of the war between India and Pakistan which gave birth to a new nation, Bangladesh. The story moves around Gustad who deals with the situation of past and present in the novel.

Time present and time past

Are both perhaps present in the future (Eliot, 88).

The above lines signify about Gustad's feelings of past and present. He sits alone and thinks about the past, his grandpa's memories always come in his mind and he feels the conflict between the past and present. His grandfather was a lover of wrestling and had given his furniture shop a name Noble & Sons. His father was an esteemed bookseller. Gustad never forgets how his father sacrificed all his fortunes for his education and his brother's alcohol.

The opening lines of the novel, *Such a Long Journey* focus on Gustad's commitment for his religion. The Parsees are very genuine and adaptive people. In the novel, in Khodadad building there are only Parsee's people who live together because of which many people tag the building with the name of Parsee building. The inhabitants of Khodadad building with Gustad Noble are Miss Kutpitia, Major Jimmy Bilimoria, Inspector Soli, Mr. Rabadi, and Tehmul Lungraa. Gustad performs his early rituals of Kusti under the neem tree which is in the compound of the building. The tree has the symbolism of a holy tree in Hindu religion. Here Mistry has expressed that this tree is a midpoint because it depicts those two religions get assimilated with each other: one is Hinduism and other is Parseeism.

Gustad wakes up at 6 a.m in the morning and he starts his prayer. It shows that he is very dedicated for his religion and wants to start his day with the blessings of God. Mistry says for Kusti: Once, twice, thrice. And thus was Ahirman, the evil one, driven away – with that expert flip of the wrists, possessed only by those who performed their Kusti regularly.Parsees have so many rituals except kusti like 'Yatha Ahu Varyo' and 'Ashem Vahoo' (SLJ,4).

The above lines signify that Mistry through his book shows a wide picture of Parsee religion by sharing the picture of the fire temples and Tower of Silence. He comments that we also are rigid for our religion and we like to perform all duties of our customs and traditions. He also says his ethno – centric community deals with certain issues of diaspora like fragmentation and identity. He himself has experienced the feeling of alienation as he is an expatriate. He is an outsider living in Canada, but he is in the periphery in India as Bharuch comments: ***"So his discourse challenges and resists the totalization of the dominant culture within India itself" (Bharuch, 1998:25).***

Subsequently in *Such a Long Journey*, Mistry has expressed the emotions and feelings of a minority community with historical events. He frames the Parsees in the picture and links the frame with historical events in the novel. The scene of Blackout paper shows the small world of Noble's family. The wall signifies that it is protecting them with the outsider people and limits their world. This wall has a height of three hundred feet. Dilnawaz says early morning, horrifying morning never, ever experienced. This line seems that at the time of war people faced many horrifying nights and days and constantly lived their life with the horrors of death. After some days with the help of one artist, Gustad changes the wall and with this inhabitant of building feel secure, safe and happy. But their happiness is short - lived and is taken away by the Municipal Corporation as they get orders from the government to widen the road by breaking the wall which makes the history of the community.

Mistry has expressed, "In Swimming Lessons", the inhabitants of Tar Gully, an adjoining space of Firozshah Baag, would be Maharashtrian in-settlers. The Parsees of Firozshah Baag think about the occupants of Tar Gully as less refined. In the story "The Ghost of Firozshah Baag", Jacqueline makes a reference to Tar Gully that all Marathi individuals are in low class Tar Gully. Jacqueline, a Goan ayah, is classified "Jaakaylee" by her Karani relatives to whom she is working. She has been prodded at the roads for her dull composition for which she answers that many individuals, like Tamils and Keralites come there with entertaining dialects and various tones, and no individuals are familiar with various tones.

In "Favorable Event", Rustomji specifies that Tar Gully has a "threatening mouth". A similar expression is utilized by Najamai in "One Sunday". Rustomji grumbles of being spit upon by a Tar Gully traveler while landing the transport. Tehmina also charges a Tar Gully's occupant of spitting upon her while heading to the Irani eatery for ice. The pride of Rustomji is scratched when his white "dugli" is ruined by the "paan" juice by Tar Gully in-traveler however done guiltlessly. Inspite of his acknowledgment that he is no better than his kindred travelers monetarily, Rustomji lashes at them finding out if they think their activity is entertaining. He calls them "uninformed savages"

From Firozsha Baag, Mistry takes us to his new homeland, Canada, in "Squatter". The protagonist of this story is shown as facing the problem of adjusting himself to the Western-style toilets and thereby undergoes severe mental agony because of it. "Lend Me Your Light" relates the story of two immigrants, Kersi who relinquishes his dream to return to his homeland and settles down as a young writer, and the other, Sarosh who fails to fit in the Canadian multicultural mosaic and takes his final flight to India.

The last tale, "Swimming Lessons", gives us the most enthralling picture of the predicament of an immigrant in Canada. Despite Canada's policy of promoting multiculturalism, the racism rife in Canada is brought to the fore through Kersi's experience at the swimming classes.

Rohinton Mistry shares a concern with the anxieties and fear of his community and we can see through his writing strategy. He deals with the past and present and his novel also recounts the history, religion of Persia and for the depiction of these terms he has chosen Gustad as a mouthpiece. He says to Malcom, that your Christianity came nineteen hundred years ago to India, but our Zarasthustra came to India fifteen hundred years ago. ***"Your son of God was born before the Buddha, two hundred years before Moses, and do you know how much Zoroastrianism influenced Judasim, Christianity and Islam?" (SLJ,4).***

The above lines imply here that we are from different religion and there are many religions in the world. All religions have different origin and history and individuals have respect for their religions and rituals. The conversation between the two signifies that Gustad has many concerns for his religion as he gives discourses on his religion to his friend, like how people are influenced and it has come many years before. Through lines we get to know it prominently that for Parsees, their religion is very supreme.

Rohinton Mistry, consequently, effectively summons a feeling of misfortune and sentimentality in the foreigner's experience and the distance of Parsees in India. Through the characters' sufferings Mistry depicts the advancement of aimless heroes joined exclusively by their own self towards an acknowledgment of humankind and obligation.

Such a Long Journey has an element which portrays before us that Persian people do not like involvement of people from other communities in their community. First, at the death of Feroze Gandhi, Dilnivaz says to Dinshawji that we all know that he has been murdered. She has doubts about it that it was not a heart attack. As we all know that he was disliked by his father– in –law, Mr. Nehru. Dinshawji agrees with her. Second, Nagarwala incident confirms that Parsees do not like any sort of involvement of others in their lives. Mr. Nagarwala belonged to their community and he was framed in a scandal of sixty lakh rupees by Mrs. Indira Gandhi. But he was supported by his own community members like Major Jimmy Bilimoria, Gustad and others.

Such a Long Journey also has some elements of hope and yearnings. Gustad is the character whose life is full of challenges and problems. His three children, Sohrab, Darius and Roshan have different problems and issues and he deals with them. Sohrab is the eldest child who is brilliant in his education. Gustad has some ordinary dreams and gets very excited when he qualifies the entrance test of IIT. He decides to celebrate this happiness on Roshan's ninth birthday but his happiness is taken away by Sohrab when he shouts, "IIT, IIT and sick with IIT, I am not going there." (48) When he refuses, it is like a situation of betrayal for him. Next challenge he faces, when her daughter falls ill with diarrhea which is a prolonged disease. Last challenge he faces when he gets a complaint about Darius by Jasmine's father Mr. Rabadi. He says that they both are having an affair. Gustad deals with all the issues in a delicate and good manner.

Mistry depicts another scene of betrayal faced by Gustad, when one morning, Major Jimmy Bilimoria disappears without telling anything to anyone. After some days, Gustad gets a parcel in their home which comes from chore bazaar. He finds a cheque of ten lakh rupees which has to be submitted in the bank. Through this parcel, he gets the information about Major Bilimoria that he has joined RAW and is involved with Mukti Bahini group. Later he gets information about him when he reads in newspaper that Bilimoria is in the jail. He has been arrested on the charges of corruption. Gustad's world gets darker after hearing this news and his heart fills with fear. He plans to make a trip to Delhi and decides to meet him. The Bilimoria and Nagarwala case is same in the novel: both worked for RAW, both get arrested on the charges of corruption and both die after this. Major is sent in imprisonment and later he dies with heart attack. His funeral takes place in Tower of Silences. After some time Gustad's another friend, Dinshawji dies with cancer. Gustad loses both his friends who depart from this world one after another.

Such a Long Journey also has the elements of poverty and depicts how poverty fills the eyes with tears. Gustad's daughter's condition worsens day by day and because of poverty, he is not able to give her proper treatment. He tries to give his best; however, he can achieve only a bit when Roshan's condition gets better. Now she can go to school and family starts feeling normal. We can say that nothing is controlled in Gustad's life, but he is the hero of the novel. He learns many lessons from his life and the real change everyone notices in him, when he permits Sohrab to lead his life on his own term.

Mistry as a writer at the end resolves all issue and gives a satisfactory end to the novel as compared to *A Fine Balance*. Roshan recovers with her illness and Sohrab comes to the home after death of Tehmul. Wall dispute also gets resolved at the end of the novel. After reading the full text, we can say that Mistry wants a good government, peace, law and order in the nation (Moss, 168). It is a documentary of the cultural ethos of Parsee. It also portrays the picture of contemporary issues which are still not resolved like politics, corruption, and regional and religious orthodoxy. We can say the novel is the tale of sufferings and struggle of Gustad. Mistry defines the difficulties of Parsees and other minorities in

India. Mistry has chosen two words to highlight his community and these are preservation and restoration. The symbols are neem tree, wall, names, buildings and blacks' stones. Mistry ends his novel with the lines of Tagore's book, Gitanjali which means that life is based on hope.

In *Such a Long Journey*, Mistry also gives some religious elements. He says that sun, river, fire and moon all are creation of God. Zoroastrian worshiped fire. Being a Parsee, Mistry is aware of all his customs and rituals of his religion. In the novel, Mistry has given some religious words like Kusti, loban, Gomez etc. which are not easily understood by non–Parsees.

The short stories in *Tales from Firozsha Baag* present the anxieties of the Parsee residents of a housing complex and they struggle with the question of self and identity. Detached from their native roots, they are unable to India as their home. Things worsen as they enter the post-colonial age and are forced to make sense of the new socio-cultural and economic environment. They lose their hope and eventually attempt to settle elsewhere. Their quest for identity is a lifelong struggle.

In addition to their identity crisis in the newly independent India, they are further pushed into confusion and fear as the 'sons of the soil' or the non-Parsee natives of the country refuse to accept them as a part of the mainstream. The othering that was practiced by the Parsees back in the colonial days as they projected themselves as the superior, racially distinct community, comes back around to push them toward the margins.

Thus, Firozsha Baag is much like ghetto complex that shelters those who may get rejected by the mainstream. Politically motivated conflicts, however, seem to be the major reason for such rejection in the present day pluralistic Indian society. The Parsee confrontation with what is called as the mainstream Indian society and the resultant decrease in the acceptance of the Parsees adds to the dilemma of the residents in Firozsha Baag. Conflicts arise not only with the outsiders but also amongst the community members.

In *Auspicious Occasion*, Mistry attempts to shed light on this show the lack of cohesiveness rising within the community members. He presents the case of Rustomji who is an educated, aged man chooses to remain indifferent to the traditions and customs of the Parsees. Similarly, the youth often rebel against the traditions and eventually abandon their cultural heritage. Sustaining the community seems a burdensome task when the younger generations continue to adopt new ways of living and question the values held in the past.

In *Swimming Lessons*, Mistry presents various personalities of the Firozsha Baag as he draws on their differences in opinions when it came to community, faith and traditions. The narrator is seen remembering his time in Bombay, the place of his birth. This brings him a lot of comfort as he is glad to know that he has a known birthplace as opposed to his cultural heritage as a Parsee that he is entirely alienated from. Mistry has deep rooted respect and love for India as his birthplace and doesn't hesitate in stating facts that present the Parsee community in a negative light. In his short story, *The Ghost of Firozsha Baag, Jacqueline, a Goanese maid hired by a Parsee family in Firozsha Baag gets her name mangled as Jaykaylee. Using the narrative of language hybridity, the writing suggests the inherent superiority complex in the residents that shows itself whenever they interact with a non-Parsee.*

The endless name calling practiced by the residents is drawn from their colonial past that put them on a pedestal and somehow justified their prejudice against the non-members of their community. The repeated usage of the term 'ghati' or uncivilized for the non-Parsees only goes to show their reluctance to let go of the colonial mindset. The author, thus, places an equal blame on both, the Parsees and on the non-Parsees when taking into account the present-day experience of alienation faced by the community members. His portrayal of the community members as the residents of the housing complex presents a clear picture of the many everyday challenges faced by the Parsees and their constant struggle for survival as a dwindling minority group.

Chapter Four

Critical Analysis of Narrative Techniques of Rohinton Mistry in Indian Context

Rohinton Mistry and Salman Rushdie both have similarities in their writings. Like Salman Rushdie, Mistry, too, uses the historical, political, geographical, religious, legal, hybrid language and economic as narrative techniques in the novel and through these he presents a clear picture of the nation to the readers. He never compares or contrasted our country with another and never merges nation with another; he just uses history of the nation as one – dimensional and secondary he uses for his narrative. He uses history as a narrative to depict a world of Parsee and in novel his main protagonist is proud of his Parsee identity and shows a respect for his culture.

Thus, if someone does a deep study of Rohinton Mistry's and Salman Rushdie's novels, then the reader can see many similarities in their writings. Both choose the same city, Bombay and create a small scene of Delhi. Mistry also took the canvas of a particular decade of history from 1965 to 1971. He portrays the scene of 1971 when East Pakistan was fighting with Pakistan for the freedom and the novel also takes a picture of politics and corruption of the nation during that period. The author has portrayed many narrative techniques in his writings and they are mentioned below.

The first technique is shown through the history of wars. The novel has many dimensions: 1948 Pakistan War, 1962 China War and the 1965 Pakistan War. These three wars presented different Parsee lives with different characters. In the novel, Major Bilimoria's character has presented the Indian Army and conflict between India and Pakistan. The China war has the significance of humiliation of India at the hands of Chinese with the central character, Gustad in the novel and this war was a failure of India's first Prime Minister Jawahar Lal Nehru. Here the author narratively elaborates the failure of Nehru's strategy and expresses that he had a blind faith on Chinese premiere Chou – En – Lai. This implies that Nehru wanted to make a friendship with China P.M and by this strategy, he planned to open a border between two nations similar to U.S.A and Canada. Indian people tagged the Chinese with the slogan of ***"Hindi – Chinese Bhai – Bhai"***. But the history has witnessed the betrayal of China. The novel sheds light on history how China broke the trust and attacked on India.

On the other hand, Mistry interlinked Gustad's life with the politics and shows how his life faced hurdles of politics as he recounts many things. Mr. Noble is a noble person just like his surname. Mistry connected the last war of Pakistan with Dr. Paymaster and has taken a good freedom fighter's name, Lal Bahadur Shastri, who had defeated the Pandit Jawahar Lal Nehru. The election contest lasted for twenty - one days and the nation got a new Prime Minister Lal Bahadur Shastri but he unfortunately died only after 18 months of his retaining the office. This narrative technique is a tremendous quality of writer which can also be easily seen in Rushdie's novel Midnight's Children.

The second technique used by the authors is that of the place where the plot of the novel is drawn. Mistry uses Bombay as a major geographical narrative and New Delhi as a minor one. New Delhi is shown in the story when Gustad goes to Delhi to meet his friend Jimmy Bilimoria in the jail. On the other hand, Mistry makes Bombay a city of Parsees margin. He has chosen Bombay in three of his novels because around seventy percent Parsees live in Bombay. He created many streets and road names in the story which gives the readers a flavor of Bombay. And the geographical landscapes are Nul Bazaar, Dhobitalao, Virar, humdrum of flora market, Colaba, Bandra and Red-light areas. In the novel, he connected these places with the road names and they all make a feel of the metropolitan city of Bombay: G.R Station, Vir Nariman Road, Mahalaxmi Road and Elphinstone Road. He also shows Bombay city as a fashionable, and tourists get attracted to this place for spending their vacations.

As Mistry has shown Bombay as a metropolitan, which is very fast forward and the inhabitants are always in a rush. Through this he says, an accident can happen frequently and narrates this with the characters of Miss Kutpitia's brother and nephew both of whom were killed in a lorry accident. Gustad also met with an accident and his hip bone got fractured. He took a rest of three months on the bed. He also depicts that Bombay too has average problems like other cities like measles, dehydration, typhoid, sunstroke, diarrhea, and chicken pox and tetanus and he also says that Municipal government has started many Pests control programmes. He narrates that both the cities, Delhi and Bombay are heaven for the diseases.

Subsequent to the narrative of geographical and historical, Mistry uses the third narrative of politics in the novel and expresses that politics is a broad term which is made by the sub-categories of religion, economic, corruption and law of India. During that period, politics mainly gave negative impact on the nation and these negative impacts are depicted by the Parsee community in the novel.

Such a Long Journey discusses the events of identity crisis through the political circle. Author has expressed that political figure has only one work which is to make the nation corrupt. This narrative directly deals with Nehru-Gandhi family with the episode of Parsee Feroze Gandhi. After the partition, the first government was formed by Nehru and his daughter Mrs. Indira Gandhi was the most corrupted character in the novel who used her political powers, did many scams with RAW to fulfill her personal affairs. Mistry's narrative works are shown very well and he depicts the scene how Mrs Gandhi dominated RAW, manipulated them and also blackmailed them. The Nagarwala conspiracy of 1971 and Major Jimmy Bilimoria are the best examples of it. They both fell in the scandal which was created by her, both of them got arrested for money scandals, both went to jail and one died mysteriously and another died of heart attack. Later she is criticized by Parsees when she orders about nationalization of Banks and demands a new state Maharashtra. The corruption was not only created by her and Nehru. She actually did all this to make the car business of her son Sanjay Gandhi successful. Mistry has shown the contrast of negative and positive political politicians: at one hand he shows Indira Gandhi, who belongs to the negative and on the other hand he shows her husband, Feroze Gandhi who belongs to the positive. He was a Parsee and died of heart attack but Dilnivaz says in one scene that he was not liked by the Nehruji from the beginning. So, all Parsees have doubt whether he really died with heart attack or he was murdered. *Such a Long Journey* gives another scenario of corruption through the Shiv Sena party of Maharashtra. This party is known as a Fascist group and they want ***"Maratha Raj"***. The party leader's personality reminds Parsees the story of Adolf Hitler and Mussolini because both were very strict and dominating in their nature. The Fascist party is same like them in their rule, arrogance and nature. Thus, Parsees feel insecure and they start thinking that now minorities have no future.

Fourth, he uses the narrative of language hybridity. The word hybridity means cross between two different cultures and identities. The principal theorists of this term are Homi Bhabha, Gayatri Spivak and Paul Gilroy. In the novel, Dilnivaz says, "What? Names get changed! What sister fuckers?" It is an act of abusive language which we normally say in the day-to-day life in fighting or frustration. Another incident happened when Mukti Bhaini news was published in the newspaper and Dinshawji asked Gustad

> ***"Have you read today's newspaper? Have you seen today's newspapers; all pictures are there? Bloody butchers, slaughtering left and right. And look at the whole world, they are completely relaxed, doing nothing. Where is maddhar chod America now?" (SLJ,76).***

The above lines imply that the words like 'Maddhar chod' and 'sister fuckers' are abusive language in Indian society because we do not use these words for our sisters and mothers but the writer shows us how the individuals were so frustrated, so they were using these words very frequently and commonly. The essence of sister fuckers is very disrespected and bad but the Parsee people were really broken by the fake promises of government. Eventually they are aware that it makes their mouth dirty only.

Fifth, he shows the narrative of flashback and nostalgia with the character of Gustad. From the beginning till end, his life is a challenge or we can say his life is a journey of pain and sufferings. It means he often goes in flashback or sees a clash between the past and present by many incidents. First, when his father's business had gone in loss, he had a plan in his mind that he would open an esteem book shop along with his son Sohrab. Second, when he was badly ill and had not got full medical aid in the past. Moreover, he couldn't be able to arrange money for her mother's funeral. Same thing happens to him in the present, when Roshan falls ill with a very complicated disease of Diarrhea and she was not able to digest even water. That time too, he was not able to pay medical bills so he sells the camera. Actually, this episode brings tears in the eyes of readers.

Sixth narrative is associated with the perspective of religion. India is a multicultural country and Mistry shows a wide canvas of religions in *Such a Long Journey*. He makes a frame of names of gods and religions in the novel through many scenes:

> *"Using assorted religions and their gods, saints and prophets: Hindu, Sikh, Judaic, Christian, Muslim, Zoroastrian, Buddhist, Jainism"*. (*SLJ*, 182)

These lines express here that he has taken names of all Gods and religions like: Lord Ganesh from Hindu religion, Jesus Christ from Catholic, Gautam Buddha from Buddhism and so on. He also takes the readers on a journey to temples, dargahs, monasteries and churchs. Mistry's narrative of religion is depicted by the characters of Ghulam and Malcolm in the novel. Both these characters come from different religions: one belongs to Muslim while other is a Christian. Malcolm is Gustad's college friend and Ghulam Mohammad is a RAW agent. With these characters the novelist again throws light on humanism because Malcolm goes to church for a prayer with Gustad when Roshan was ill and Ghulam protects Parsee community through RAW. Through this we can learn that all Gods are one, only names are different.

Seventh is the narrative of friendship and benevolence. Actually, friendship is like a key which not only makes a strong bonding between the humans but it can also help make friendship between the human and animals. Here I want to give an example by my own knowledge of author. Jonathan Swift's Gulliver Travels novel is a good example about the friendship and benevolence because this novel depicts the friendship of protagonist Gulliver with the horses. They are animals who have been shown with an ability to speak and listen. To live with them Gulliver also learned the concept of friendship and benevolence with them.

In the novel, it is about Ghulam, friend of Jimmy Bilimoria, who took an oath at his death that he would take a revenge of this. He said that he had become a victim of corruption and illegal system. He was innocent and did not get any justice. Mistry tries to clarify his innocence through the scene of conversation between the Gustad and Malcolm and says:

> No one was ready to believe him, he said there was something very fishy about the whole thing, they said. (*SLJ*,207).

The meaning of lines here is that Jimmy Bilimoria was tortured very badly in the jail. When Gustad came to meet him in the jail, he talked about the third degree torture of police. He assumed that he might die with such treatment. The Court or law does not show any reaction on this. Mistry's narrative here shows the actual reality of politics which depicts that rich and politicians can buy and control anything. Eventually, they can give birth or death to anyone.

Eighth is the narrative which deals with education at many incidents in the novel and, presenting into sub-sections. First, when Miss Claudina, Principal of Roshan School, sheds light on the scene when refugees came in the nation for shelter because they were being killed by West Pakistan. They were being harassed as Pakistan burnt their homes also. This scene gives the feeling of fear to the students. Second incident that vouches our notion is when student came for studies from other cities. They come from a different origin, some are weak, while some are intelligent and bright. Here Mistry presents Indian Institute of Technology at the center, where students came to get better education. IIT is a brand and Government institution. It only gives admission to those students who are very intelligent in their area of interest. Mistry also connects this association with the eldest son of Gustad, named Sohrab. He got admission there and this news becomes a festival for Gustad. It can be news of celebration for any ordinary man because IIT is the most reputed institute in India and a famous education institute all over the world. Students make tireless efforts for years to grab this opportunity. Sohrab's luck was favoured him, and he is intelligent too. Gustad wanted his son to become a world-famous scientist. With these scenes, Mistry also portrays the middle – class family who always first think about their children's education, ambitions and career. Third incident is the picture of uneducated persons. Gustad's Christian friend Malcolm, who is a musician, is unable to earn his bread and butter. At last, his earning starts with the municipal job and he explains his job to be shitty and boring. He recalls the days, when western music was very popular and in demand.

Last narrative depicts the Parsee faith on Zoroastrianism. Mistry's narrative style in the novel also enlightens about the customs, traditions and rituals of the Parsee. All the characters of the novel who live like a family unit in Khodadad building perform their duties towards their culture. The names of the characters show us the Parsee faith on their religion: Gustad Noble, Miss Kutpitia and Pastakias, they all give the feelings of Parsee identity. The Kusti prayer is performed by Gustad early morning under the tree of Neem for the Ahura Mazda. Ahura Mazda is the supreme God in their religion and he is the creator of the heaven on earth. Gustad has so much faith in God that he christens his children from the Persian epic, ***"ShahNameh"***. The name, Sohrab is the legendary name of this epic.

Mistry also narrates the death rituals of Parsee. When Tehmul dies in the Morcha then his dead body is carried to his flat by Gustad. A priest performs prayers of *Yatha Ahu Varyo* five times and he also performs other rituals like washing the sandalwood with oil and leaving it on the flame. The significance of these prayers is that they want to fill the room with the fragrance of sandalwood and give a peaceful adieu to the dead person. The cremation procedure is different from that of other religions. Leaving the dead bodies in the Tower of Silence to fill the empty stomach of crows is no way similar or associated to any ritual of any other religion or sect.

Subsequently, they all were the major narrative techniques of this novel but now I want to discuss some other things. *Such a Long Journey* also shows that Parsees are very introvert in nature and they do not feel the need to mix with other peoples. When Gustad decided to celebrate birthday of Roshan, he invited only two people: one is Dinshawji and other is Miss Kutpitia because they both are Parsees. It is really true that they are introvert. A movie on Parsees' lives and marriages has been made in Bollywood with the name, ***'Shirin Farhad ki Toh Nikal Padi'*** which was released in 2012. The movie shows how Parsees have different ideology regarding their marriages and they only like to marry in Parsee community The movie is a good example to learn the prominent study about them.

Mistry also uses his narrative with the flavor of food, shown with the help of family of Noble. He shares what kind of ingredients they use and what they cook. Some of the Parsee foods are

"Kutchoomber of onion, coriander, hot green chilies and Dhansak". When Roshan's birthday party was being celebrated, the guests were served Parsee food like a vegetable stew made of carrot, peas, potatoes, cumin and ginger. This dish has a salty and spicy taste. Another dish was made of ***"rice with cloves"***. The Parsee fish curry with rice is very famous and it is easily available at many restaurants of Bombay. They have a different taste about their foods. They like to eat ***pappud*** or ***paapad*** with their meal to enhance the taste.

Such a long journey has some elements of the social ambience of Parsee culture and customs. Mistry has given a lot of education and knowledge about their religion and rituals. So, in his debut novel, he portrays the picture of Parsee in a very prominent style. His narratives in the novel are very straight, his characters lives are modest and they try to achieve the best life in the political air. He has made a plot on history and politics and then linked it with sub – plots which mainly deal with the inhabitants of Khadadad building. He shows how they struggle and cope with these things. Some learn the lesson from that while some prefer to move away in other direction. Mistry shows his religion because he wants the readers to be aware of it. Like Salman Rushdie, he also makes history which we call past linked with the present. This is a narrative technique which is often used by diasporic writers.

A Fine Balance (1995) is Mistry's second novel. The perspective about Parsees starts with *Such a Long Journey* and followed in his next novels. Again, Mistry depicts Indian frame with subjects of geographical, intellectual, discrimination, religious and legal. The novelist also shares the heterogeneity on a wide canvas with his characters associated to different professions viz. students, servants, tailors, peons, textile workers and lawyers. *A Fine Balance* is filled with different flavours of religions and caste – like Hindus, Muslims, Sikhs, Parsees, Chamars, Bhungis, Thakurs and Pandits. His narrative has used characters of different age groups and sexes in the novel. The novel begins with the partition of India in 1947 and ends with assassination of Prime Minister Mrs. Gandhi and Sikhs riots followed just after that. The geographical narrative covers the land; it means rivers and landscape from the village, thrashing crowds and sea by the metropolitan city. He did not directly take the name of any place but encompasses the beauty of India in the novel. He has used many narrative styles by showcasing many incidents and some of these are described in the following section.

First, the storyline of the novel mixes well with the historical incidents of the nation. The author chooses partition of 1947 and throws light on the aftermaths of the partition. He applies the same narrative as in *Such a Long Journey* and captures the partition of India by many methods without including any international event. He divides the novel between the village and city and enlightens how historical incidents had given bad impact on the characters' lives. Riots had given the day – and- night curfew, violence and bloodshed. Everything is shut down during and after riots whether it is an educational institution or a place related to business. With incidents like riots, not only working class suffers, but students also face issues regarding their studies. Mistry has set a very good example here with the Parsee characters, Nusswan and Dina. When the curfew has forced, Nusswan gets tensed with financial losses due to curfew, his sister Dina could not go to school and sits at home for many days on the other hand with a fear of death in riots and partition. Muslims were worried of their appearances; hence they cut their beard. On one side, city people faced riots and on the other hand, people of village faced caste discrimination. Mistry's narrative of partition is not only interlinked with the city; he also connects it with communalism in villages. Mistry shows a balanced picture in his novel. On one side he shows riots against Muslims and in the contrary to it draws a picture of friendship between Muslims and Hindus with the example of Ashraf and Dukhi. At the time of riots, Muslim inhabitants not only cut their beard but they also changed their shops' names to save their occupation and lives of the family. When a group of twenty Hindu people came to shop of Ashraf, he and his shop got saved as his shop was named as Om and Ishwar. They said that the shop belonged to them and they prove it by lowering down their pajamas to show their Hindu skin. *A Fine Balance* connected the division of sub-continent in a dramatic style with the perspectives of class division, religions and geographic.

The second narrative of geography includes the entire land of India and connects the city to the village. Mistry has described both, city and town in a very well manner and continue by commenting that cities are metropolitan and have big buildings, crowded streets, fashionable lightings, big cars, air-conditioned buses, library with music, restaurants, hotels and big shopping malls. Comparison to a city, a town is full of fresh air and greenery, wells, electric lamps and villagers. In rural area, they can buy oil and other groceries by exchanging it with wheat like in a barter system, it means wheat sometimes works like money. Mistry says, if you talk about vehicles in villages then there is no car; villagers travel on bullock carts and lorries. He also shows the landscapes of hilly mountains and river not to express the beauty of India, but he connects it with Maneck Kolah. His father, Mr. Kolah lost a huge portion of agricultural land at the time of partition. According to him, the lifestyle of a town is also different from a city. In towns, food is cooked on traditional *chulha* (furnace), while in cities, food is cooked on modern *chulha* and oven. Sometimes it is made by international ingredients which may give different types of stomach disease and said, in the contemporary world, these landscapes are also filling with the poison of developmental strategies. He presents another example of Mr. Kolah; though he is living at a hilly place, still he becomes a patient of colon cancer which was common among ordinary people in the modern era. He has vastly defined geographical beauty of India, but he did not give any name to them.

Third is the political scenario of *A Fine Balance* which deals with the Emergency of 1975-77 and Sikh riots following the death of Mrs. Indira Gandhi. Mistry also depicts this political scenario with inhabitants of town and cities. Mistry has encompassed the multi-dimension canvas of Emergency. First, he depicts the characters who become victim of Emergency. Second, he shows the horrible picture of Emergency, third, the banners and slogans and the last, the newspapers report about the Emergency.

The fourth narrative talks about the groups of different caste and religions. Mistry gives a vivid picture of internal Emergency through these castes and religions. He gives the view of the heterogeneous crowd to the readers and uses the narrative of caste, class and religion barriers. In the novel, Avinash tells his friend Maneck about the Emergency:

> 'Three weeks ago, the High Court found the Prime Minister guilty of

> cheating in the last elections. Which meant she had to step down. But she began stalling. So, the opposition parties, student organization, trade unions – they started mass demonstration across the country. All calling for her resignation and later she declared a state of Emergency'(*AFB,* 245).

The above lines imply that Dina Dalal, the protagonist of the novel has a different view about the Emergency. She said that it is a game of power and politics about which everybody knows, but she is totally shameless and her attitude is same like before. On the other hand, her brother Nusswan has a positive feeling about Mrs. Gandhi and the Emergency. He said through this our nation will be reformed with the concept of ***"renaissance"*** and the sterilization family planning programme will control the rising population. Mrs. Gupta also agrees with Nusswan, and gives her point of view that Emergency will soon recover the nation from bad habits. But Dina and youth had different points of view about it.

The fifth narrative gives the events of corruption going through during the Emergency. Emergency makes human not only corrupt but also heartless and inhuman. The narrative of Emergency portrays the dominant scenario through lifeless objects: the banners and slogans which are posted on the wall for Prime Minister. She demands for peace, co–

operation, hard work and discipline from the nation. Many banners and slogans give a positive side to sterilization process. The time of Emergency was very disheartening and she demands peace in the period of violence and riots but nothing works. The situation gets worse and it is depicted by many scenes. First, when Avinash dies, his body looks so horrible; his nails were missing, he had burn marks on his chest and cheeks. Second, the forceful sterilization of uncle and nephew, Om and Ishwar's castration ended all hopes of their marriage and at last, they become beggars. Third, the poor children of slums ran with a rally of Mrs. Indira Gandhi for food only. So, we can say that this novel also highlighted the act of brutality.

Sixth narrative narrates the turbulence of the nation with the assassination of Mrs. Indira Gandhi. Mistry first uses Avinash to narrate the Emergency, now he uses a taxi driver to give an account on the scenario the after death of Mrs. Indira Gandhi. The taxi driver started his narration with poor and old homes vanish, forcibly "sterlization" means nasbandhi. He said the world is now divided between Hindus and Sikhs because her followers are killing innocent Sikhs to take revenge. This is a true picture about the riots as many innocents get killed during riots, many women lose their husbands, kids lose their fathers and many leave their roots and become refugees in some other city or country. It all depicts how the innocent citizens have flown their blood without having any fault.

The seventh is the economic and financial – crisis narration in the novel by choosing the poverty as a theme with the characters Dina Dalal and Chamars, Om and Ishvar. When Dina is not able to give the rent, she is harassed by landlord Ibrahim. Ibrahim is a man who used to bully her and always makes an eye on her to take her advantage. The novelist here sheds light on difficulty of getting accommodation in a metropolitan city. He also discussed the issues of unemployment and beggars of the city, said just because of rising prices, the beggar's master sells the dead bodies of beggars to the agent to give them normal funeral. These all-harsh pictures show the roots of corruption in the city.

Subsequently, comparative to the city, towns are also poor and everyone deals there with the poverty. Here the Misty gives his perspective on the class conflict between the upper class and lower caste (untouchables). He narrates how Dukhi who belongs to the chamar caste that basically comes under the Harijan community, in modern context it is referred to the SC community, dukhi is the character who always tries to break the old orthodox chain. He decides to make his children tailor and tells them that they would not continue the profession of cobbler which has been imposed on them by the society. He sends his children Narayan and Ishvar to the town to earn bread and butter. Later Narayan reconstructs his house and marries Radha without taking any dowry. Mistry here conveys a message to the readers through Narayan and Dukhi who belong to the lower caste but their dreams and mentality are very modest. They had an urge for better life. So, Mistry says that we should not be orthodox and if one wants to do better in life, we should encourage and support them to enhance their upcoming life.

Eighth narrative is about the domination, subjugation and oppression by Brahmins, Thakurs and Pandits. They are the upper strata of the society and they murder Narayan and his family brutually. Here author narrates how the upper caste dominates the lower caste and silences the screams of untouchables by killing them mercilessly. When Narayan wanted to cast his vote to his community candidate, he gets brutally killed by Thakur and his goons. It is a bitter fact that caste system is still present in the 21st century in each and every form whether it is related to education, marriage and so on.

Last narrative makes some parallel dimensions about religions like *Such a Long Journey.* There are so many characters in the novel who belong to different religions. Ashraf is a Muslim, Mrs. Gupta is Hindu, taxi driver belongs to Sikh community and Dina and Maneck are Parsees. The other two characters who are also hindus but they are identified as untouchables Om and Ishvar. Same as in *Such a Long Journey,* Mistry talks about Parsee customs of Tower of Silence. ***Here he has given the information to the readers about the Parsee festival, Khordad sal and Navroze (AFB, 43).*** The all four protagonists of the novel are religious and, if we look *Such a Long Journey,* it begins with the prayer scene. *A Fine Balance,* he enlightens the readers with another custom of Parsees and that is a wedding ceremony. This is shown through Dina's wedding with Rustom which is being held on ***"Fire Temple".*** So, the novel has same narratives and readers learn about many customs of Parsees after reading the novels.

These were the major narratives and now I want to shed some light on one more narrative that has been depicted by the author in his novel. Misty portrays the scenario of Indian secularism in the novel with the concept of religion. Characters like Dukhi, Om, Ishvar, Narayan, Ashraf Chacha and Mumtaz played this scene. The untouchable Dukhi sends his children to learn tailoring under guidance of Muslim Ashraf. Ashraf and Mumtaz have been like second guardians for them and Ashraf's family was protected by them at the time of riots and during Narayan's wedding Ashraf and his wife serve the Chamar guests with etiquettes and hospitality. This kind of relations not only shows secularism, but also presents a picture of reciprocated love to each other that is completely neglected in modern era. We are educating ourselves day by day but love is getting vanished from the hearts completely because people do not value sentimental values, they only using one another for their own benefits only.

A Fine Balance also talks about the narrative style to depict the law and order in the nation. He has the main concern of Internal Emergency because it was the time when all fundamental rights were suspended and humans were becoming insane and inhuman to each other. This is expressed through many incidents: first, when Rustom dies in an accident and the culprit never gets arrested; second, when Ibrahim's landlord abuses Dina for the rent third; when Thakur Dharamsi killed Narayan mercilessly and burnt his family alive in their home; fourth, no one is arrested for this heinous crime; fifth, Avinash was missing and police did not file an F.I.R of missing; Forcibly sterilization of Om and Ishvar, MISA Act. These all incidents depict the scene and corruption during the Internal Emergency and this is the real picture of emergency which had made conditions worse.

A Fine Balance also depicts law and order with a positive aspect associated with some characters while with a negative aspect with some others. It means some people were loyal to their profession and some were taking advantage of it. Mistry has shown this incidence with Dr. Shroff and his son, Nusswan. Dr. Shroff has chosen to serve the poor and needy persons in the village, leaving a luxurious life in the city. On the other hand, his son Nusswan is getting worried about his financial losses when the nation was facing curfews and violence. Mistry also chosen to give a comprehensive account on education. He depicts this scenario with a conflict between upper – caste and untouchables. He says that in villages, education belongs only to the upper strata of the society. When Ishvar and Narayan were watching the students in the classroom, they both were caught by a teacher who makes a biased comment on them. "You shameless donkey! I will break your bones". Another incident happened, when they again come to the school and were harshly beaten by the teacher. Yes, this is true that education that at time was only available to the upper – class people and the only work for untouchables was to serve the Pandits and Brahmins.

Here, I want to give a good example from my knowledge on Dalits Dr. Bhim Rao Ambedkar belonged to scheduled caste. He was born into Chamar caste and history witnessed that peoples behaved rudely and disrespectfully with him. He had to sit outside the class and could get education only through the voice of the teacher. Though he belonged to the lower strata, but his name is written in golden letters in history. He took sixteen degrees and is considered to be one of the highly educated and respectable people in the world. He is a God figure for the lower strata of society who broke the chains of caste taboos. He made the constitution law for scheduled caste people and gave them the legal right to education and moreover with the rights of equality and liberty. If we look at his image in the 21st century, in 2016 his birth anniversary was celebrated by U.N.O and in 193 countries. Eventually, four protagonists come from different social backgrounds and through the journey of the entire novel they, at last, learn how to live with peace and love in the political situation. The Mistrian novel highlighted very sensitive issues like caste and community. On the subject of caste, he says that it is not a part of one village, city and mountain. He also throws light on some other delicate issues which are still prevalent like sati, dowry, begging trade, problems of widow. He connected these subjects with the characters in the novel. Dina becomes widow when her husband Rustom dies in an accident. She chose to live independently and his brother dominated her. When husband died then the widow had to be sati at the time of cremation. Begging was dealt with Om and Ishvar, after the sterilization they were neither a man and nor women so they become the beggar at last. So, these are extreme sensitive issue and it happen every day in many cities.

Such a Long Journey is a bit contrast in comparison to *A Fine Balance* on one of the narratives. Mistry does not show his main concern about Parsee community as he deals with many communities in this novel. *Such a Long Journey* has main focus on Parsees but in his second novel he also shows Chamars, Brahmins, Sikhs and Muslims. *A Fine Balance* has encompassed the vastness and complexities of India as his narrative is talking about the murders, suicide, terror, naxalites, caste, violence, brutality and stories of corruption. Through these, Mistry depicts how the common people deal with tragic circumstances. This situation sometimes gets uncontrolled and the victim may commit suicide. Maneck Kolah is an example here, who commits suicide after being bullied incident by his seniors. Mistry portrays the two-dimensional picture and with his expressive writing he not only connects his characters but also the listeners and readers to the incidents and characters.

In *Tales from Firozsha Baag*, a collection of 11 short, interconnected stories represents the dilemma of the Parsees in residing in Bombay who find themselves struggling with their own identity and position in the newly independent state of India. Having held important social ranks during colonial times, the diaspora community is left in a state of doubt and confusion as change seems to be the only constant. Living in the city of Bombay, the characters of Mistry's stories present the anxieties of a religious and ethnic minority that is left to find its road to survival. The rapidly changing social environment often pushes the characters to the edge of change as well. While some are seen holding onto the values and traditions of their past glory, others seem to take the leap of faith and adapt to the new norms. There is a never-ending struggle to balance the new and the old way of Parsee life. Mistry explores the various relationships at the heart of the Parsee community, the cultural identity, as well as the uniqueness of their community living, while also highlighting the syncretic nature of the diasporic Parsee experience be it in North America or India.

The narratives presented through the course of the book are suggestive of the author's deep understanding of the Indian Parsee experience, state of transition, and everyday struggles. With wit and wisdom Mistry looks at the Parsee life in the 80s through a critical lens. In a review of *Tales from Firozsha Baag,* Amin Malak observes, "The writer's sympathies preclude his condemning or disowning his culture in its entirely, and the humorous rendition of character and incident makes the criticism poignantly effective and lasting".

Mistry uses the narrative of location to outline the importance of Bombay as a city of endless opportunities as well as, as the city that sheltered a considerable number of Parsee migrants. While Bombay seems to be the Indian home for the migrant community, yet the residents of Firozsha Baag display a deep sense of longing for a place they can truly embrace as home. Facing a range of challenges brought by the rapidly changing social conditions of post-independence India, the residents are confined to their ghetto-like housing complex. The author thus takes into consideration the negative aspects of the city as experienced by members of minority groups. In *Tales from Firozsha Baag,* initially one observes the status of Parsees as global citizens, as the stories and characters move between India and North America and between Bombay and Toronto all while concretizing their status as migrants, regardless of the location. The final story of the book, *Swimming Lessons* represents Mistry's life as a Canadian immigrant from India and his struggles with the question of communal identity. The stories set in North America present a sense of a complete loss of identity due to double displacement. This identity crisis rising from shifting locations is one of the important themes of the book. Mistry has used the narrative of the economic status of the Parsees to highlight the range of the economic conditions of the community members. Contrary to popular belief, not all Parsees can be classified as the upper-middle class. Thus, not all the characters in *Tales from Firozsha Baag,* who are categorized as the middle class can afford conveniences like refrigerators, and owning a car is certainly not the norm.

From the 1960s to the 80s, there was a socialist sentiment that made access to imported goods and luxury items difficult. The consumer items were mostly scarce and came with quite a price tag. In Mistry's *Tales from Firozsha Baag* refrigerator becomes an object of much trouble for Najamai. She is the only person to own a refrigerator and her a lot of unwanted attention.

While the author has draws on the diverse economic conditions of the Parsees, yet there seems to be an inherent superiority complex drawn from the colonial glory and is well carried by most of the community members who don't shy away from name-calling the non-members. The mistreatment of the poor is also highlighted in one short story, *The Ghost of Firozsha Baag,* as the Goanese ayah suffers at the hands of the Parsee masters. Still identifying themselves as the colonial elite, the community members are stuck in a colonial hangover.

Through the narrative of language hybridity, the author has shed light on the frequent practice of domestication of English by the Parsees. In *The Ghost of Firozsha Baag, the maid's name is mangled by the house owners and Jacqueline becomes Jaykaylee.* This bears witness to the problematic acceptance and application of English and how the strange was often familiarized before it was accepted.

Furthermore, it is observed that the usage of Parsee terminology by Mistry adds to a holistic linguistic experience, as well as represents his appreciation and longing for his own cultural identity in a faraway land. Uma Parameswaran points out, "Mistry has bolstered the India-in-Canada reality by confidently using Parsee words without either glossary or textual explanations such as resorted to by earlier writers of Commonwealth Literature".

Another narrative of rites and religion follows the ethnoreligious detailing of a few important days of observance in Zoroastrianism. Through this narrative, the author has explored the two contrasting attitudes held by the residents when it came to traditions. An *Auspicious Occasion* the female protagonist, Mehroo decides to hold on to the rituals and traditions of Behram Roj, that is the Zoroastrian New Year. Mehroo's husband, Rustomji, thinks of these traditions as a thing of the past that have lost their meaning. Interestingly, Rustomji is several older than his wife.

A narrative is also built on grounds of education and gender roles as Rustomji presents the case of an educated Parsee man as opposed to his submissive wife who is quite the conformist. Mehroo abides by all the customs of the Parsees while Rustomji doesn't see any relevance in them. He doesn't let Mehroo stay in a separate room when she's menstruating although it is a customary practice. Yet, despite his rejection of age-old traditional practices, Rustomji doesn't part from his chaotic ways and Mehroo continues being a part of their decaying household. This leaves the reader wondering if Mehroo would've stood up for herself had she been just as educated?

The short story *Condolence Visit* also presents a similar situation in which Daulat Mirza; a widow decides to cope with the loss of her spouse on her terms. To her, the traditional mourning rituals are futile and superficial. She decides to leave a lamp lit in her husband's room beyond the prescribed days as it brought her peace and comfort. Further, she gives away his clothes in an orphanage and his turban to a young groom.

The above-mentioned stories shed light on the burdens of tradition and the driving force behind communal changes, that are individuals themselves as they consciously choose what is the best for them.

Mistry builds a narrative on the phenomenon of family disintegration throughout the course of the book. Loneliness, alienation, and the disintegration of families are observed as residents of Firozsha Baag bid farewell to their young kids who leave for the first world, in hopes of a better life. In *Condolence Visit* Daulat Mirza is heartbroken from the loss of her spouse and gets annoyed at another resident Najamai when she visits. However, she pulls herself together as she realizes Najamai's good intent. The latter is a lonely resident whose daughters have left for abroad. This loneliness cripples several characters in the stories. Mistry's writings bring to light the reluctant attitude that the residents have toward the larger Indian society and the maladaptive patterns of behavior that encourage the younger generations to leave whenever they can.

Furthermore, the author describes the burden of double displacement. In the story, *Squatter, a* young Parsee man in Canada named Sarosh, struggles with his bowels each morning as he is forced to climb up the toilet seat. He can't get his bowels to function normally in a seated position even after 10 years of trying. He returns to Bombay and can no longer bring himself to feel at home. He experiences the same loneliness he felt in Canada. This parallels with Rushdie's creation of characters that don't feel at home, regardless of their location, and are subjected to live at the peripheries. *Squatter* and other stories, that are set partially in Canada display a "periscopic vision" of the diasporic writer comparable to Salman Rushdie in this critical essays, *Imaginary Homelands.*

Westernization and cross-cultural narrative are built around the conflict faced by the characters individually and collectively. The experiences of the characters through the course of the novel suggest a declining moral and ethical value system as the young residents turn to materialism. The continuous exposure to changes in the social climate in a post-colonial India pose a threat to the Parsee identity, as younger residents turn away from their traditions abandon their heritage. The loss of cultural identity coupled with the dwindling population of the Parsees becomes an alarming cause of concern. Cultural exchanges with the members of other community also threaten the survival of this religious minority.

As the young residents in Firozsha Baag join in a rebellion against these age-old traditions and several others who moved face the aftermath of a double displacement, an identity crisis develops. The author explores this crisis through his characters. In *Lend Me Your Light,* the protagonist,

Kersi, who has moved to Canada feels like he's stuck with a dual identity. In the same story another character, Jamshed only sees hopelessness in India, and moves in a quest to find financial opportunities and attain the cultural superiority of the West.

In another short *The Swimming* Lessons, the author uses the narrative of nostalgia. Kersi finds himself all alone in Canada, unable to adjust to the new life. He takes swimming lessons and gets ridiculed by three young men. He develops a pessimistic attitude and constantly feels like he's being labeled as the 'other'. Although he feels alienated yet he doesn't return to Bombay as he doesn't associate his cultural identity with India. Thus, he turns to nostalgia and finds comfort in thinking of Bombay as his birthplace.

A change of perspective is introduced by the author as one of his stories as he switches the narrator to a non-Parsee in the story, *The Ghost of Firozsha* Baag. Jacqueline, the narrator of this story, is hired as a help in one of the houses in the residential complex. The author uses her character to give an outsider's perspective on the lives of the residents of Firozsha Baag.

Overall, this research on Disaporic experiences in Rohinton Mistry's *Such a Long Journey, A Fine Balance* and *Tales from Firozsha Baag,* discovered that the novels are very symbolic in nature as *Such a Long Journey* showcases the journey of Gustad's life in a suitable and presentable format.

From beginning to end in the novel, he suffers a lot and learns many lessons through his journey. On the other hand, *A Fine Balance* signifies that nothing in the life is in a proper balance. We all know that life is imbalanced and we spend our whole life to make a balance according to our necessities and circumstances. Sometimes we are successful in achieving this and sometimes we fail. The *Tales from Firozsha Baag* present the case of a residential complex in a post-colonial Bombay wherein the residents face a range of everyday challenges while trying to understand their communal and individual identities.

Chapter Five

Critical Anaylsis of Rohinton Mistry's Work in Indian Context

Rohinton Mistry has arisen as a considerable essayist on the world artistic scene. He is an exceptionally famous individual from Indian diaspora. He involves a critical situation as an Indian diasporic essayist. As of late there has been a boundless development of interest in his works. The connection among writing and life appears to be the object of expanded consideration in his works.

Rohinton Mistry has a place with that class of the Indian creators who moved their base from India to elsewhere yet for the duration of their lives they keep missing their mom land. Mistry was profoundly propelled by Indian foundation, Indian individuals and their brain science and that is the reason he has expounded really on his Indian experience prior to going to Canada. He draws his significant wellspring of material from the noticed life in India.

Mistry's works are particularly nostalgic. It is Mistry's undeniable longing to return to his underlying foundations nostalgically that tracks down its numerous articulations in his anecdotal world. Over the span of portrayal, he envisions India in its multi-layered intricacies and real factors. As per Mistry it was his sibling Cyrus who caused him to understand that it isn't important to expound on New York or Paris to be a fruitful essayist. Bombay is adequate for that.

Despite the fact that Rohinton Mistry is referred to wherever as a Canadian essayist, Canada barely includes in his composition. He decides to return to his unique home, city and culture instead of detail the foreigner experience. In a meeting; he examines why he expounds on Bombay, the working-class Parsee in Bombay, the world he has abandoned:

Going to Canada, confronted with the truth of making money and understanding that despite the fact that I had, up to that point in my life, read books and paid attention to music that came from the west, there was much more associated with living in the west. I felt entirely OK with the books and the music, however living in the west made that equivalent music appear to be significantly less important. It abruptly got back to me obviously the way that I was copying something not mine, that look bad as far as my own life, my own reality (Narmeen Shaikh, Interview with Rohinton Mistry).

Mistry's anecdotal composing incorporates *Tales from Firozsha Baag, Such a Long Journey, A Fine Balance* and *Family Matters*. Stories from *Firozsha Baag* is Mistry's first assortment of eleven interrelated brief tales that unites a portion of Mistry's most punctual and best composition. It was first distributed in Canada in 1987 and a reproduce named *Swimming Lessons* and Other *Stories from Firozsha Baag* turned out in 1989. The equivalent was additionally distributed in UK in 1992. This first assortment of Mistry denoted the appearance of a colossal ability. Here the majority of Mistry's later subjects and distractions might be found in small.

Every one of the accounts of Tales from Firozsha Baag are set inside one apartment building in Bombay. Here is a magnificent prologue to the inhabitants of Firozsha Baag. The stories detail the everyday existences of the inhabitants of the previously mentioned high rise. They manage working class life among the Parsee people group and the issues of their regular daily existence. Like other working-class people in Bombay the inhabitants of Firozsha Baag need to take part in day-by-day fight with irregular water-supply, weather beaten homes, stripping paint, falling mortar and spilling rooftop. These phenomenal stories offer us a chance to go into the day-by-day schedule and cadence of their lives, and when we arrive at the last story we are as acquainted with individuals of Firozsha Baag as we are with our own neighbors. The swarmed, pulsating life of India is splendidly caught in this series of stories.

Stories from Firozsha Baag was heartily welcomed by pundits and general peruses the same for its bits of knowledge into the perplexing existences of the Parsee occupants of Firozsha Baag. This assortment inspects the idea of shared and individual personality according to a Parsee viewpoint. These accounts cover an expansive scope of subjects and tones. Here ***'Mistry utilizes the account procedure of memory and recalling'. (Jaydip Singh Dodiya, 2006)***

Stories from Firozsha Baag comprises of eleven stories – One Sunday, Auspicious Occasions, A Ghost of Firozsha Baag, Condolence Visit, The Collectors, Of White Hairs and Cricket, The Paying Guests, Squatters, Lend Me Your Light, Exercisers, and Swimming Lessons. All through the eleven stories, the significant characters return as repeating figures loaning a feeling of relational association among the occupants of Firozsha Baag. A storyteller—regularly thought to be the most self-portraying hero of Mistry's compositions—presents the occasions and subtleties of the characters' battles to discover their personalities in the postcolonial 'new' India, just as workers' endeavors to adjust to their new universes in places like Canada.

> **A born story teller, in his tales Mistry depicts middle class life among the Parsi community, as he recalls it from**

> **abroad. All his eleven intersecting stories are set in an apartment block in** Bombay **where a number of Parsi families live: all the people who live there are, in turn, the protagonists of one or more short stories. The author himself tells the last one, thus revealing that he comes from Firozsha Baag, too.**
>
> Silvia Albertazzi

Rohinton Mistry's presentation novel, *Such a Long Journey,* is inexactly founded on a progression of genuine occasions that occurred during the Indira Gandhi organization. Short recorded for the renowned Booker Prize, *Such a Long Journey,* Mistry's first novel, oversees splendidly to depict Indian culture and day to day life setting it against the background of the subcontinent's unstable postcolonial governmental issues. This political background is the material whereupon the upset existence of Gustad Noble and family is worked out. He is the undisputed hero of the book. Mistry expertly gives the significant occasions in India those in the private circle of the Noble family and of the other significant characters in the book.

Bombay is the setting of *Such a Long Journey.* Here, notwithstanding, the social conditions that gave a far-off background to the brief tales currently bear upon a specific Bombay family. Here Mistry manages the Parsee climate in India. The activity happens in 1971 in Bombay exactly when war breaks out among India and Pakistan. The book got the Governor-General's Award, the W.H. Smith/ Books in Canada First Novel Award, and the Commonwealth Writers' Prize for best book. Haldar Santwana is of the view:

> *Such a long Journey is the first novel written by Rohinton Mistry, a writer of Indian Diaspora, who settled in Canada. Though the novel was published sixteen years after Rohinton Mistry had settled in Toronto, it has no trace of Canada. Rather, it reveals the author's deep concern for the Parsi's in India in particular, and for the development of post-colonial India in general.*

Haldar Santwana

Such A Long Journey is a many-sided story of the victories and debacles of a merciful bank representative's loved ones set in India in 1971, a period of homegrown disturbance and battle with Pakistan. Set during that year's contention with Pakistan, the original concerns a Parsee man, Gustad Noble, who works at a bank. In this clever Mistry has investigated top to bottom the different complex credits of Parsee life, history, culture and character, as he recalled these from the Canadian diasporic space.

Mistry set this novel at a delicate point in contemporary Indian history, when the period of

Nehru had quite recently finished after his unexpected passing, and before long offered approach to decline legislative issues of advantage, nepotism and brutality. Further, during the period 1962-1972 India needed to take part in three progressive conflicts with China, Pakistan and for the freedom of Bangladesh. This period additionally saw the ascent of shared governmental issues, the rise of new political arrangements and the lethargic yet sure legislative issues of votes by the prevailing Hindu/Brahmin people group of India. The outcome was the underestimation of more modest gatherings and ethnic minorities.

Silvia Albertazzi puts the plot of this novel as such:

> In Bombay, in 1971, Gustad Nobel is a Parsi bank clerk and a family man. He has two children, Sohrab, a university student, and Roshan, nine years old, and a loving wife. His life is shattered when he receives a letter from an old friend, Major Jimmy Billimoria, requesting him to receive a package for him. This letter does not only plunge Gustad at the core of a complicated political situation, but is itself harbinger of disaster. His son leaves home after quarrelling with him over the young man's refusal to go to the Indian Institute of Technology. His daughter falls ill. The municipal

> government requisitions the land where his apartment stands in order to widen the road. And last but not least, the contents of Billimoria's package put at risk Gustad's job at the bank. During the chaotic times of the Bangladesh war, family order is disrupted and Gustad has to find a new way to look at reality and cope with the outside world.

Silvia Albertazzi

A Fine Balance is Mistry's work of art. It is his subsequent book. It was distributed in 1995. It won the second yearly Giller Prize and Commonwealth Writers Prize. Simultaneously it was short recorded for the 1996 Booker prize. This rambling work set up Mistry as a prominent author. In its reach and all-encompassing quality, it is practically identical with Vikram Seth's *A Suitable Boy* and Shashi Tharoor's *The Great Indian Novel.*

There is a depiction of India in *A Fine Balance* from different headings. It is about the sufferings of the four characters because of political impedance particularly during crisis period. Dina Dalal, a Parsee widow, Om and Ishvar, two untouchables and Maneck an adolescent from line of India are the significant characters. The novel is set against the foundation of 1975 yet it likewise talks about the historical backdrop of India for the 75 years.

Om and Ishvar are the untouchables portrayed in the book. While portraying these characters the writer has taken occasions before the Independence of India. Mahatma Gandhi's thoughts regarding untouchables, their sufferings and the privileged society are distinctively portrayed in the book. The writer says that the abominations towards the untouchables proceeded even after Independence. It was at its top during the crisis. Mistry has made an honest effort to introduce the pitiable state of occupants of the ghetto spaces of Dharavi and Kurla.

A Fine Balance manages the sufferings and troubles looked by everyday person in India. It tells how four characters – Dina Dalal, Om, Ishvar Darji and Maneck Kolah – meet up to live in the frenzy of Bombay. The account portrays their experiences with their heaps of hardships and agonies. Mistry has picked characters from minority and stifled networks. In each character India might be found. Fellowship of this load of characters shows how individuals in India figure out how to live in a particularly pivotal and vomited condition. Maneck addresses youth of India who shares how adolescents in India were smothered during crisis. Avinash, a companion of Maneck, an understudy chief, is killed dubiously. Maneck's life is upset by the passing of Avinash. Maneck goes to the train station, his reality broke. He leaves the tracks as an express train moves toward the station and ends it all by allowing the train to run over him. Self-destruction on a rail route track is normal wonders in India.

Indian family fondness and neighborliness is uncovered in A Fine Balance. Maneck goes to Dina's home as a paying visitor and acts as though he is her child. Maneck is uprisings against his dad since he would not like to assist his with fathering in business. Be that as it may, Maneck's dad doesn't need maneck to proceed with the privately-run company. Similarly, Ishvar needs Om to get hitched however Om declines. Yet, basically he consents to wed. Dina first won't live with her sibling Nusswan yet later, she is accommodated to him. One can track down a sort of Indian family liking among the minor characters. The personality of Ashraf uncovers the Hindu – Muslim fellowship. Narayan and Ishvar save Ashraf's family from revolting Hindus.

The Emergency straightforwardly affects the existences of the four primary characters of the book. Practically every one of the significant characters are influenced because of crisis. Dina and the tailors' business run reasonably flawlessly for close to 12 months, yet impacts of the Emergency trouble them frequently. The shantytown where the tailors reside is wrecked in an administration's beautification program and the inhabitants are uncompensated and compelled to move into the roads. Later Ishvar and Om are gathered together by a police bum attack and are offered to a work camp. Following two months in the camp they pay off out with the assistance of the Beggar Master. Ishvar and Om are fortunate and Dina chooses to allow them to remain with her. The tailors and Dina discover inconvenience from the landowner since she should be maintaining a business from her level. She imagines that Ishvar is her significant other and Om their child and furthermore get insurance from the Beggar master.

Ishvar and Om return to their town to discover a spouse for Omprakash who is presently eighteen. Maneck likewise gets back. He accepts a rewarding position in Middle Eastern Dubai. Dina, being separated from everyone else now, and her defender the Beggar Master having been killed, has no insurance from the property manager who needs to break her loft's lease control and charge more lease, so she is expelled. Dina is compelled to again live with her sibling, Nusswan.

Omprakash and Ishvar return to their old town Ashraf Chacha gives them a spot to remain while they look for marriage possibilities for Om. Ishvar and Om become the survivors of constrained disinfection. The vasectomy happens. After vasectomy they experience the ill effects of disease.

After eight years, Maneck gets back interestingly from Dubai for his dad's memorial service. Maneck is shocked by the viciousness that trails the Prime

Minister's death, for which Sikhs are killed. He gets back and goes to the burial service. While at home he peruses old papers and discovers that Avinash's three sisters have hanged themselves, unfit to bear their folks' embarrassment at not having the option to give endowments to their relationships. Stunned and shaken, he chooses to visit Dina in Mumbai for better news. He gains from Dina the terrible lives that Ishvar and Om – one incapacitated and the other emasculated – have driven as vs after their town visit. As Maneck leaves, he experiences Om and Ishvar in the city. The two previous tailors are almost unrecognizable on account of their rottenness, and don't seem to review him. They say 'Salaam' as far as he might be concerned, yet he doesn't have the foggiest idea what to say and strolls on. After at some point, he ends it all.

What social and political conditions mean for the working class and the minimized local area is featured in this book. The existences of four principal characters specifically, Dina Ishvar, Om and Maneck, are intertwined. They attempt to defeat their obstacles however neglect to keep a fine equilibrium. It is a cognizant work to embrace a greater amount of the social truth of India. It is significant to understand that Mistry's depiction of Hindu culture is certifiably not a fair ethnographic record of Indian culture. He proposes that distinct shameful acts are inborn in the act of standing. The savagery of unapproachability is seriously censured as an adding to a disintegration of significance in the existences of Dukhi, Narayan, Ishvar and Om. A model for the cold-bloodedness and assertion that describes their treatment by their betters is outlined in the accompanying manner:

The news was the same type that dukhi had heard evening after evening during his childhood; only the names were different. For walking on the upper-caste side of the street, Sita was stoned, though not to death- the stones had ceased at first blood. Gambhir was less fortunate; he had molten lead poured into his ears because he ventured within hearing range of the temple while prayers were in progress. Dayaram, reneging on an agreement to plough a landlord's field, had been forced to eat the landlord's excrement in the village square. Dhiraj tried to negotiate in advance with Pandit Ghanshyam the wages for chopping wood, instead of settling for the few sticks he could expect at the end of the day; the Pandit got upset, accused dhiraj of poisoning his cows, and had him hanged.

A Fine Balance: Rohinton Mistry

The focal point of *Such a Long Journey* is metropolitan Bombay, the Bombay of dreams and bad dreams, of expectations and despondency, of delight and enduring, of comedies and misfortunes. It is the Bombay Mistry had known as a kid and an adult, and the manner in which the city goes through change. However, Bombay, as is introduced in the novel is likewise one which had been made and created by ethno-strict minorities; the structures, the organizations, the milestones and the general person of the city, all stand observer to this multi-social person of the spot. It is then that one can comprehend the later solid perspective on the city, which become the capital of Maharashtra, and consequently tried to be assumed liability for by the Shiv Sena. It is this that gets a confrontationist thought of having a place, a politically charged environment that lies behind the account essentially. In any case, regardless of all his polemical legislative issues concerning whose personality is undermined or is dissolved, Mistry has the sympathy and the wide perspective to praise every single part of Bombay. Mistry's Bombay is as yet the celluloid capital, of the lilt of well-known music chiefs, the Carnival's line, swarmed Bombay of extraordinary assortment and conceivable outcomes.

At one level, the novel dominates in fascinating insights concerning Bombay markets, roads, foundations, celebrations and other notable perspectives. We discover a wide range of stirred up ceremonies and works on, cutting across Hindus, Christians, Parsis, Muslims and others discovering place in the story. Mistry gives a ton of reality to portray the English language to send his own motivations. A few styles and tongues, types of discourse taken from Gujarati, Marathi and different dialects are spoken, to debase the supposed immaculateness of the English language. This is, as is notable, a vital component of post-provincial journalists as well, who have Indianized the English language to acquire neighborhood tone, local and ethnic character in their works. Mistry doesn't spare a moment to utilize filthy subtleties to uncover the soil and foulness of Bombay. A brief look at life of chawls can be found in Mistry's *A Fine Balance*:

> The tap is out there, in the middle of the lane. Most convenient. You won't have to go far for water, like they do in other inferior colonies. This is a nice place.' He swept his arm around to take in the field. 'Newly developed, not too crowded. The rent is one hundred rupees per month. In advance.' Nawaz tapped the walls with his fingers like a doctor examining a chest, then stamped his foot on a floor plank, making it wobble. He made an approving face. Well, built', he whispered to the tailors.
>
> Navalkar gave a circular nod. 'We have even better huts. You want to see? 'No harm in looking', said Nawaz. They were led behind the rows of tin-and-plastic jhopadpattis to a set of eight brick-walled huts. The roofs once

> again were of rusted corrugated metal. These are two hundred and fifty rupees per month. But for that money you get a pukka floor and electric light'. He pointed to the poles that fed wires to the huts, pirated from the street- lighting supply.
>
> *A Fine Balance:* Rohinton Mistry

Chapter Six

Conclusion

In the conclusion, the exploration of this research expresses that the study of diasporic experiences in Rohinton Mistry's *Such a Long Journey, A Fine Balance* and *Tales from Firozsha Baag* uncovers the experiences about the belonging, identity and quest for the identity of migrant's soul in every angle. It provides future scope for the readers. Each case of the study of diasporic experiences reflects how the post–independence time, emergency, corruption, politics, discrimination, past and present time etc. leave readers with many questions regarding the migrants, their lives and experiences in general which can be concluded as follows.

First, every aspect of the study of diasporic experiences attracts individuals to better understand that writings of the 1980s to 1990s have experimented historical, political and social upheavals. In the experimentation, the novelists of this period have narrated and re–narrated the stories of their own religion and community with the perspective of diasporic experiences.

The reflection prolongs as migrants are viewed as an issue in modern and post–modern literature and the readers try to understand whether they are nostalgic or not. They are migrants but their veins are filled with the blood of India so they always choose to write about their nation. They choose literature to express their feelings with different dimensions of society as society is always born with differences of mind. A society can never learn the ideology of equality.

At the same time, the research focuses on how the study of diasporic experiences in *Such a Long Journey*, *A Fine Balance* and *Tales from Firozsha Baag* has an essential element of identity. They are so many issues in the novel which speak directly and indirectly about the identity and quest for identity. India is a country in which many people are divided on the lines of classes and castes, religions, and languages. Caste and religion affect the people and social institutions and as an outcome of this, the society is filled with disaffection.

Rohinton Mistry depicts the broken images of humans under the cultural and socio-economic grounds. The suppression of untouchables in the society is an act of inhumanity. He uses history as a backdrop in the novels but does not portray history as an obsession in any manner. He displays towns, hills and valleys greatly with the context of geographical attributes. The study about these issues with the concept of self-identity as a recurrent theme is correlated with the title of this book.

The three novels conclude that they are dealing with the theme of identity. In *Such a Long Journey* one observes the concept of the self-identity. In *A Fine Balance* the concept of search for identity in the polluted atmosphere of politics and corruption takes the center stage. *Tales from Firozsha Baag* explores the slow but steady loss of identity faced by a community of middle class parsees and the everyday challenges they face in retaining the same in the metropolitan city of Mumbai. All the characters in all three novels have the quest for identity.

In *Such a Long journey,* the self-identity perspective is mainly talking about Gustad and his life experiences, sufferings, journey, pain etc. from beginning to end of the novel. When street and colonies names were getting changed, the name of Lamington Road becomes Dadasaheb Ambedkar Marg. He feels that his identity is lost now. This act, for him, is loss of identity. It can be true for anyone because loss of old names is like loss of social tradition, social identity and self-identity.

It was, for him, about the loss of childhood which shows me and many other critical thinkers that it has a significance role. According to Mistry, Gustad lived his life as a king in his childhood and was deeply attached to his mother. But after the death of his mother, he felt uncomfortable with everyone in the world. This shows a man who has a desire of past feeling in the present world. This is a loss of present and paternal identity. He compares his paternal identity with that of his son, Sohrab and says he will not consider him as his son until he learns to respect elders. He says at the time of Sohrab's refusal for IIT admission that you will also feel loss of childhood in future.

When the wall is being broken by the municipal workers, he makes many attempts to save the pictures of gods and goddesses on the wall. At last, he loses the wall with the death of Tehmul, a retarded child. This thrills his body and a feeling of fatherhood starts coming in Sohrab. He puts the child in his arms and learns that he cannot achieve anything in present life with the memories of past. On the other hand, at the death of Dinshawji he does not shed a single tear because he thinks crying of man is a symbol of weakness in the society. So, the title of the novel and Gustad's life is interlinked and complementary to each other under the searching identity concept.

On the other hand, Mistry's second novel *A Fine Balance* is about the search for identity and it is portrayed by his characters. His four unlike characters mingle with each other and want their self-identity in the society which is totally polluted. Dina's character is liberal and she is a victim of suppression, patriarchy of her brother from her childhood. She lost everything in her life, first her father and later her husband, both of them dying in accidents. Ultimately, she opens her boutique with his coworkers Om and Ishwar.

Emergency breaks dreams of all the characters and she is forced to go to her brother's cage and lose her independence. Here she not only loses her freedom but also her self-identity because earlier she was an independent woman. On the other hand, the characters of Om and Ishwar are also searching for identity in the fast metropolitan city. Their ancestors belonged to lower strata of society and were also victims of the caste system in India. As Dukhi, the father of Ishwar does not want to continue the profession of shoe-making, he sends them to the city to break the orthodox chain. This is also a forward step of untouchables to search a new identity. They start their earnings with Dina but they do not have complete trust on her. So, they try to get a direct order from companies. They face lots of problems to adjust in a metropolitan city. I want to say that they do not have any identity in the village and in the city as well.

Subsequently, the sterilization incident during Emergency makes their situation worse. Om is attaining the age of marriage but he becomes impotent after sterilization and on the other hand, his uncle Ishvar loses his legs and becomes handicapped. At last, they are compelled to become beggars losing their identity and other charms in their lives. The character of Maneck loses his identity when the government passes a law to connect the city with the hilly areas. He thinks now hilly areas will be full of crowds and pollution due to heavy transport and his essence of nature will vanish. So, the place and people related to it will lose their identity too. Here I want to say that characters in *A Fine Balance* are getting identity crisis in various aspects.

Tales from Firozsha Baag takes into account the dilemma faced by Indian Parsee families residing in a metropolitan city. It describes the various challenges pertaining to identity and religion faced by the residents of the housing society. Being exposed to a rapidly changing social environment, the families struggle to uphold their traditional values while trying to make sense of their new social standing in a post-independence India. While the members of the older generation are largely strict about their cultural heritage, the younger people are more liberal and ready to embrace the changes brought in by the waves of westernization and cultural exchanges.

As some characters stray from their traditional ways, as seen in *The Exercisers* and *The Condolence Visit,* they are met with harsh criticism. The conscious rejection of older ways coupled with growing ethnic and religious doubts seem to lead the residents towards a state of perpetual state of hopelessness. They seem to have lost their sense of belongingness and cannot associate with the term home or homeland.

Furthermore, as members of a minority community, they struggle to find their place and become end up assuming the role of the 'other'. Such exclusion and conflicts with the majority places them at the periphery of Indian society in a quest to find better opportunities and the hope for greater acceptance, the youth end up moving to other countries, such as Canada and the United States only to bear the burden of double displacement. The characters face the overwhelming loss of communal identity. This mirrors the author's own life as an India Parsee and a Canadian immigrant.

There is no solution to these issues and we cannot reach somewhere to conclude it. *Such a Long Journey* mainly talks about the Parsee community and their identity during reign of Mrs. Indira Gandhi in India and her politics. *A Fine Balance* is an advanced level of the first one. It deals with many Indian issues during post-colonial time which are somehow ignored by many Indian writers. Both novels have the same element and structure of politics, history, corruption and casteism related to the Parsees. Mistry's writing shows how his community struggles with their situation. Still the community is dying and moving towards extinction because humanity is dying.

Nevertheless, the study of diasporic experiences in novels assumes a precious part about exploitation and subjugation. Mistry raises a high voice against lack of humanity. If we see his characters, they are mercilessly exploited. No one shows any concern for them and in 21st - century caste system is still present. He says that in our society rich is becoming richer and poor is getting poorer day by day. He uses his writing as a weapon against exploitation and exploiters.

Indeed, today's youngsters have so much concern for the study of diasporic experiences because its impact is fresh, alive and relevant in today's time. Regardless of the coming of contemporary writing, the study of diasporic experiences is remarkable and unique in relation to different sorts of scholarly fiction from multiple points of view. At the same time, diasporic experiences in Rohinton Mistry in *Such a Long Journey, A Fine Balance* and *Tales from Firozsha Baag* transcend the generation of migrants on these stories.

In this way, diasporic experiences of migrants remain to be significant even today and will remain so in the future. Besides, the indigenous information and knowledge found in diasporic experiences say that diaspora is not only for migrants who are leaving their own roots. It is also related to the individuals who become victims of the disparity between majority and minority. They also have the feeling of dispersed. The individuals who leave their homes, cities and villages for better perspectives like, education, career etc. in their life, they also feel alienated. Mistry sets many examples in the novel like Maneck, Om, Ishvar etc. who hail from different castes and become victims in the hands of people from majority groups. People have their own mindset which will take a long time to change. They set many derogatory and specific names for another caste, community and minority like scheduled castes are achhoot, Muslims are mulle, Sardaars as baarah, North-East people as Chinki-Pinki and much more. This not only affects their feelings but it also affects their soul.

Besides, this work shows the clear and recurrent theme of the identity of dispersed migrants. All through the eras, the situation may change but the core shows the diminishing of values explicitly. The diasporic experiences of writers work as a tool to educate society on the most proficient method to live respectably and gently with others.

Moreover, the given statement reflects society's nature on these delicate issues. I attempt to put forward many questions in my research and answers to these questions. Society is made by people and we all are a part of it. We are the only one who can change the mindset of individuals. According to me, all are educated, mature and we all have the same blood. We should not dominate others and give them a feeling of alienation and nostalgia on any terms. Mistry also says that everyone must understand each other's feelings, live equally and should be liberal with each other.

This research also enables individuals to learn friendship and benevolence in real life. It gives lessons to overcome diasporic issues in general. It also frequently inspires energies and comforts the youngsters.

Finally, the study of 'Diasporic Experiences in Rohinton Mistry's in *Such a Long Journey, A Fine Balance'* and *Tales from Ferozshah Baag* enables to think about the migrants, dispersed peoples and their feelings. From these, Mistry conveys a paramount message to readers and learners. He emphasizes on values for worldwide citizenship, respect for each other, humanity, generosity, love and benevolence. Besides, he embodies a prominent attitude like we should not only respect individuals but we should also respect their culture and customs. Only then, they will feel equal and assimilated in the host country and will be able to find their hidden identity in another country.

Apart from all its major future scopes, the present research has certain limitations because due to lack of space and time many certain areas could not be touched, such as globalization, different social system, etc. At the end, it is hoped that this will encourage much more similar researches in related domain.

Bibliography

Primary Sources

- Mistry, Rohinton. *A Fine Balance*. New York: Faber and Faber Ltd, 1995. Print.
- Mistry, Rohinton. *Such a Long Journey*. New York: Faber and Faber Ltd, 1991. Print.
- Mistry, Rohinton. *Tales from Firozsha Baag*. Canada: Penguin, 1987. Print.

Secondary Sources

- Bharucha, Nilufer E. Robinton Mistry: Ethnic Enclosures and Transcultural Spaces, Jaipur Rawat Publications, 2003.
- Bhautoo-Dewnarain, Nandini. Rohinton Mistry. *An Introduction New Delhi:Cambridge University Press,* 2007, Print.
- Cohen, R. *"Rethinking "Babylon": iconoclastic conceptions of the diasporic experience."* New Community 21 (1995): 5-18, Print.

- ——— *"Diasporas and the nation-state: from victims to challengers."* International Affairs 72 (1996): 507-20, Print.
- ——— Global Diasporas: An Introduction, London: University College London Press,
- Dodiya, Jaydipsinh Ed. "The Parsi Community in Such A Long Journey". *The Fiction of Rohinton Mistry: Critical Studies.* New Delhi: Prestige Books, 1998.
- Goldberg, David Theo. *Multiculturalism: A Critical Reader. USA:* Blackwell Publications, 1996.
- Hutcheon, Linda, Marion. Richmond. *Other Soltitudes: Canadian Multicultural fiction.* Toronto, 1990.
- Jagdish Batra, Robinton Mistry. *"Identity, Values and Other Sociological Concerns"*. New Delhi, Prestige Books.
- Jaydip Singh Dodiya, *"Perspective on the Novels of Rohinton Mistry"*. New Delhi: Sarup & Sons, 2006. p.31.
- Malak, Amin. *"Tales From Firozsha Baag."* Canadian Literature, 119. Winter 1987.
- Manvar, Twinkla B. "Rohinton Mistry's Such a Long Journey: A Thematic study". *Parsi Fiction* vol.2, Novy Kapadia, Jaydipsinh Dodiya, R.K. Dhawan. New Delhi: Prestige Books, 2001.

- Mistry, Vijay. *"The Literature of the Indian Diaspora: Theorizing the Diasporic Imaginary"*, New York, Routledge. 2007.
- Parameswaran, Uma. *"Literature of the Indian Diaspora in Canada". An Overview,* South Asian Canadians. Ed. Jameela Beegam and Maya Dutt. Madras: Anu Chitra, 1996.
- Refer to Rohinton Mistry's interview with Dogmar Novak in Other *SOLITUDES: Canadian Multicultural Fictions,* Hutcheon and Marion Richmond, Toronto, Oxford University Press, 1990.
- Ross, Robert L. *"Seeking and Maintaining Balance: Rohinton Mistry's Fiction."* World Literature Today. Spring 1999.
- Rohinton Mistry, *"A Fine Balance"* (London: Faber and Faber). 1995. pp.161-162.
- Rohinton Mistry, *"Such a Long Journey"* (London: Faber and Faber). 1991. pp. 9-11.
- Selvam, *Humanism In the Novels of Rohinton Mistry,* New Delhi: Creative Books, 1990.
- Vertovec, Steven. "Three Meanings of "Diaspora," Exemplified among South Asian Religions." *Diaspora: A Journal of Transnational Studies,* vol. 6 no. 3, 1997, pp. 277-299. *Project MUSE,* doi:10.1353/dsp.1997.0010.
- Silvia Albertazzi. *"Robinton Mistry in a companion to Indian fiction in English"*. Pier

Pialo Paolo Piciucco, New Delhi: Atlantic, 2004. pp. 276-281.

- Verghese, Jose. *"Home as a cultural construct in Rohinton Mistry's Short Stories"*, Roy, Anjali Gera Roy & Meena T. Pillai, *Rohinton Mistry (An Anthology of Recent Criticism)*, Pencraft International, 2007.